The Wit and Wisdom of David Attenborough

The Wit and Wisdom of David Attenborough

Chas Newkey-Burden

First published in Great Britain in 2023 by Gaia, an imprint of
Octopus Publishing Group Ltd
Carmelite House
50 Victoria Embankment
London EC4Y 0DZ
www.octopusbooks.co.uk

An Hachette UK Company
www.hachette.co.uk

Distributed in the US by
Hachette Book Group
1290 Avenue of the Americas
4th and 5th Floors
New York, NY 10104

Distributed in Canada by
Canadian Manda Group
664 Annette St.
Toronto, Ontario, Canada M6S 2C8

ISBN 978-1-85675-526-9

A CIP catalogue record for this book is available from the British Library.

Printed and bound in UK

Illustrations by Matthew Hollings

Typeset in 9.9/16.2pt Plantin MT Pro by Jouve (UK), Milton Keynes

3 5 7 9 10 8 6 4 2

This FSC® label means that materials used
for the product have been responsibly sourced.

DISCLAIMER:

Sir David Attenborough has not endorsed and
is in no way affiliated with this book.

Contents

Introduction

Sir David Attenborough is many things – all of them wonderful. He is a broadcasting titan, whose passionate, semi-whispered narration of the natural world has been adored for generations. He is also an environmental warrior who has delicately shown us how we have harmed our planet and what we can do to make it right. Along the way, he has rightly become nothing short of a national treasure – a charming, adorable and admirable grandfather figure for generations.

He joined the BBC having only ever watched one television programme, but his matchless broadcasting career has now spanned eight decades, setting an extraordinary standard for all to follow. Initially told his teeth were too big to appear on screen, he has rarely been off it, passionately documenting the natural world and gently encouraging us to regard it with more respect. Along the way he has himself become, in the words of Louis Theroux, 'a species that is increasingly endangered and all the more precious for that'.

He has written books, been invited to address prestigious conferences and raised awareness of environmental causes. The recipient of several BAFTA (British Academy of Film and Television Arts) awards, two knighthoods and a universe of species named after him, he has also won the hearts of a nation and beyond, becoming a precious part of the fabric of our lives.

Of course, other people have enjoyed long and successful careers in television, and he is not the only person to advocate for the natural world. What sets Attenborough apart is his endless supply of charm and wit. His dry sense of humour, elegant turn of phrase and self-deprecation warm our hearts. And who could fail to be won over by his boyish enthusiasm, which has never left him, even as he reached his nineties?

As we'll see, colleagues have many fond memories of him. They remember him lying in a damp field in France, digging up worms from the ground at 10pm. When a large bird once knocked him off his feet, he lightly reprimanded it, saying: 'Now, now.' Confronted by a group of cannibals in the jungles of Papua New Guinea, he strolled closer to them and politely said: 'Good afternoon!' He charmed them, too.

Continuing to broadcast deep into his nineties, he has never complained about the strain of work. Instead, he said: 'I can't believe I've been as as lucky as I have.' Despite his colossal ability, prestige and influence, he plays it all down, saying: 'I just point at things.'

If he won't celebrate himself we will have to do it for him. So this book is a timely celebration and 'tour' of a national treasure. We will tell his remarkable story in the best way possible – through the wit and wisdom of his words. With stories and facts helping to shed light on the life of this extraordinary man, it will also include richly deserved tributes and anecdotes from his colleagues, family and fans.

I'm a lifelong lover of animals and now a writer and campaigner on animal rights and the environment, so Sir David's passion for nature has always chimed with me. I've dived deeply into the archives of this remarkable man and emerged clutching the very best facts and stories. Sir David has had no say in what I've selected as he is in no way affiliated to or involved in the book.

Blending his quips galore with his powerful messages on the environment and future of the planet, I will showcase everything that is great about Sir David Attenborough. His producer said: 'There will never be another David Attenborough.' He's probably right. So let's celebrate the one we have.

Timeline of David Attenborough's Life

1926

David Attenborough was born on 8 May 1926, in Isleworth, Middlesex. He was the middle of three sons: his elder brother, Richard, became an actor and director, and his younger brother, John, became an executive in the car industry.

He was raised on the campus of University College, Leicester (now the University of Leicester), where his father was principal. He developed a keen interest in the natural world during his childhood, collecting stones, fossils and newts.

1936

Along with his brother Richard, he attended a lecture by conservationist Grey Owl (Archibald Belaney) at De Montfort Hall, Leicester, and was 'bowled over' by his message, which has influenced him throughout his life.

1945

After having attended Wyggeston Grammar School for Boys in Leicester, Attenborough won a scholarship to Clare College, Cambridge, where he studied zoology and geology, graduating in Natural Sciences.

1947

He was called up for national service in the Royal Navy and was stationed for two years in North Wales and Scotland.

1949

He took a job editing children's science textbooks for a publishing house.

1950

He married Jane Elizabeth Ebsworth Oriel.
The couple went on to have two children.
He also applied for a job at BBC radio.
Although his application was rejected, he was
offered three months' training at the corporation.

1952

Attenborough joined the BBC in a full-time
television position.

1954

He received his big break when he was switched
from his director role to fronting the live studio links
when the presenter of the nature documentary *Zoo
Quest* fell ill. Over the course of seven series, the show
visited far-flung locations, including Sierra Leone,
Indonesia and Guyana.

1960

He returned to studying with a part-time post-
graduate degree in social anthropology at the
London School of Economics.

1963

He presented *Attenborough and Animals*,
his first children's series.

1965

He enjoyed a major promotion when he became
controller of BBC2.

1969

Attenborough was promoted again – this time to
director of programmes for the BBC.

1972

He won the Royal Geographical Society's
Cherry Kearton Medal and Award, the first of
many honours he would receive in his life.

1973

He resigned from his post as director of programmes
to write the TV series *Life on Earth* and continue
as a freelance programme-maker. He travelled to
Southeast Asia to film *Eastwards with Attenborough*.

1979

Life on Earth was launched.

1983

He was elected a Fellow of the Royal Society.

1984

The television series *The Living Planet* was launched. He was awarded an honorary Doctor of Science from the University of Cambridge.

1985

He was knighted by Queen Elizabeth II for services to television, becoming Sir David Attenborough.

1988

He was awarded an honorary Doctor of Science degree from Oxford University.

1990

His new TV series, *The Trials of Life*, was launched, to look at animal behaviour through different stages of life.

1997

His wife Jane died after suffering a brain haemorrhage.

2005

Attenborough was awarded the Order of Merit by
Queen Elizabeth.

2013

He had a pacemaker fitted but it did nothing to slow
down his busy approach to life.

2014

At the Natural History Museum in London,
Attenborough used CGI to bring his favourite
extinct animals back to life, in *David Attenborough's
Natural History Museum Alive*, a documentary film
which aired on New Year's Day on Sky One.

2015

Sir David was interviewed by the US president,
Barack Obama, at the White House. During the
conversation they discussed climate change and its

impact on future generations. In the same year, he underwent surgery for a double knee replacement.

2022

The United Nations Environment Programme recognized Attenborough as a Champion of the Earth 'for his dedication to research, documentation and advocacy for the protection of nature and its restoration'.

In the same year, he was knighted a second time, with the Prince of Wales bestowing upon him the Knight Grand Cross. And he grabbed a Lifetime Achievement Award at the 43rd News and Documentary Emmy Awards.

2023

Showing no sign of hanging up his walking boots, he presented the series *Wild Isles*.

1
The Making of David Attenborough

Early years

The remarkable story of David Attenborough began when he was born on 8 May 1926. This means he appeared in the world the same year as the future Queen Elizabeth II, and, 'like the Queen, he has become a symbol of stability in a turbulent world', said a profile in *The Guardian*.

However, he once gave short shrift to an interviewer who raised the proximity of his birthday to the Queen's. 'An awful lot of people were born around that time,' he said. 'They didn't stop producing.'

*

When Attenborough was born, it was quite a different world. George V was king, Stanley Baldwin was prime minister, the average weekly wage was around £5 and the BBC was less than four years old.

Britain was in the middle of a general strike, called by the Trades Union Congress. Many things we take for granted now had not been invented then, including sliced bread, cinemas, televisions, bubble gum, ballpoint pens and jet engines.

When he was born, women had been allowed to vote for less than a decade, and a single woman couldn't have her own bank account, or even buy a house. There were two billion people alive in the world at the time, compared with more than 7.8 billion at the time of writing.

*

David's parents married in Paddington, London, in 1922. His father, Frederick Levi Attenborough, was born in 1887. His grandfather, Frederick Augustus, was a baker and grocer from Nottinghamshire, and his grandmother came from a weaving family. Frederick junior pursued an academic path and was a fellow of Emmanuel College, Cambridge. It was there that he met Mary Clegg.

Clegg had education in her very blood. Her father, Samuel, was a school headmaster, and her grandfather, Alexander, had also taught, moving in a different direction from his father James, who had worked as a power-loom weaver in Bolton in 1861.

Attenborough's first memory is of 'a staircase' in the family's home in Isleworth, where he spent his early years.

*

Although his father had been a don (a member of the teaching staff) at Cambridge, he had moved to a new job as principal at Borough Road College (later the West London Institute of Education) in Isleworth, where he stayed for seven years.

'He got fed up with privilege, I think really,' speculated his son. 'He thought the Oxford and Cambridge system was a hotbed of privilege . . . he couldn't stand being a don anymore and he took this job and brought order to a rather revolutionary gang of students.'

★

His mother was a talented pianist and Sir David also took up the hobby at the age of about seven.

A natural education

Sir David believes that an interest in nature is not uncommon but is something we are born with. 'I think that every child born is interested in the world of wildlife,' he said, 'and by the age of four, they are still interested.'

One of the first creatures that fascinated him was a slug, of all things. 'What were those funny things?' he remembered thinking. 'How can it eat? What does it feed on? How does it even move?'

★

From the solitary slug, a passion was born and Attenborough never stopped being bewitched by creatures and nature. In 2019, he looked back at his childhood and told an interviewer that his passions

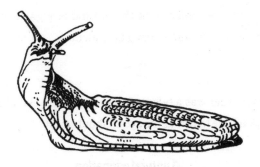

then were 'keeping tanks of tropical fish' and 'venturing across northern England on his bike as a young teen, alone, in search of fossils'.

*

Attenborough has said: 'Fossils have fascinated me for as long as I can remember.' He recalled that, as a boy, he spent much of his free time 'collecting the ammonites that are abundant in the Jurassic limestone in the countryside around Leicester'.

'The excitement of hitting a block of stone with a hammer and seeing it fall apart to reveal a beautiful coiled shell 50 million years old is as great to me today as it was when I was a small boy,' he said.

However, he believes that changes in society have made it less likely that the children of today will grow up like he did. 'As a child, I was interested in fossils, newts and butterflies,' he said. He regrets that such passions are less widespread among the youngsters of the 21st century. 'All kids have that potential,' he said, but 'the problem these days is that they have little chance of encountering these things. The United Nations tells us that more than 50 per cent of the world's population is urbanized.'

★

As many a frustrated parent will tell you, lots of young boys have untidy bedrooms, and Attenborough's was no different. However, the clutter in his childhood space was not the stereotyped blend of football posters, computer games and comics. Instead, it was an early sign of the passion that would stay with him for life.

'For as long as I could remember my brother had this strong affinity with the natural world,' said Richard Attenborough, recalling that his younger brother's room was always 'cluttered with snake casts, dead insects and the conglomeration of fossils he insisted on carrying back from our holidays in Wales'.

So, what sort of boy was David? Richard remembered 'Dave' as 'the quiet, studious one' and 'the undisputed favourite son of my academic father' – a contrast to himself, the 'noisy elder brother, the show-off with the bad school reports'.

★

After about seven years in Isleworth, David's father, Frederick, became principal of University College, Leicester (now the University of Leicester), and the family moved to College House, on the campus. David was then aged five.

*

David joined the Scouts and has fond recollections of the experience. 'I remember my time as a Wolf Cub very well indeed,' he said. 'We learned a lot of useful things and had a great deal of fun.'

Wolf Cubs is the second-youngest section of Scouting operated by the Baden-Powell Scouts' Association; it comes between the Beavers and the Scouts. Wolf Cubs are usually aged about eight to eleven years old. The skills David learned there will have come in handy during his decades roaming in the outdoors.

*

It was at Leicester, when he was 11 years old, that David first realized he could make a living from animals, after he heard that the woman who ran the zoology department needed a supply of newts for her laboratory.

He suggested to his father that he could provide newts for threepence a go. The cunning source of his supply was a pond just five yards from the laboratory. No one at the university was aware that his newt supplier was so close to home. Had he not been so interested in nature he might have had the makings of quite the entrepreneur.

★

Attenborough returned to the Isleworth area in January 2020, to open an exhibition of work by the artist J M W Turner, who had lived in nearby Sandycoombe Road, Twickenham, in the early 19th century. The exhibition was held in the artist's newly restored home, which opened in 2020 as Turner's House.

Looking back on his early childhood in the area, Attenborough admitted he'd had no idea such a renowned artist had once lived nearby. 'You could walk up and down Sandycoombe Road all your life and never know that this was once the place of one of the great geniuses of 19th-century painting,' he said.

★

In 2023, an interview with Attenborough was conducted to form part of an exhibition about his life. The exhibition, 'The Attenboroughs at Leicester', was in the Digital Culture Studio in the David Wilson Library at the University of Leicester. It included a series of trinkets from Attenborough's life, along with a photograph from his university days and items from his Scouts group.

★

David's younger brother, John, was a boss at the Italian car manufacturer Alfa Romeo. He died in 2012, having been diagnosed with progressive supranuclear palsy, a late-onset degenerative disease.

★

His older brother, Richard (who became a life peer in 1993), was an Academy-winning actor and filmmaker. Among the films he appeared in are: *Brighton Rock*

(1948), *I'm All Right Jack* (1959), *The Great Escape* (1963), *Doctor Dolittle* (1967), *10 Rillington Place* (1971) and *Jurassic Park* (1993).

★

Attenborough is therefore a 'middle brother'. The 'birth order' theory holds that the order you were born in has a profound and lasting effect on psychological development.

Five theories about the 'middle child' include:

They're competitive.

They're peacemakers and people-pleasers.

They want to fit in.

They are independent and they focus on friendships.

They misbehave to get attention.

We will leave you to decide how many of these relate to Britain's national treasure.

★

The architect who designed Haydon Hill House in Bushey, Hertfordshire – where David also spent time as he was growing up (though he didn't live there) – was Decimus Burton. One of the most celebrated architects of the 19th century, he was the man behind the Wellington Arch at London's Hyde Park Corner, London Zoo and the glasshouses at Kew Gardens.

★

Some boys look up to footballers, rock stars or movie stars. Attenborough had different idols. Growing up, he regarded Captain Scott, the Antarctic explorer, 'as a hero', he said. Scott's final diary entry, which read, 'For God's sake look after our people', was 'the epitome of the British spirit and heroism', Attenborough said.

He continued: 'People always talked about the conquest of Everest and the conquest of the poles, and it was a matter of national pride that you man-hauled your sledge to the South Pole.'

He remembered his own adventures, including the 'gurgling brook and the kingfisher and the bulrushes and the stars of white crowfoot or marsh marigolds or buttercups'.

'That's the landscape I grew up in as a child,' he added, 'as are the ponds I sat by, and so I do think fresh water is sweet.'

*

Speaking of early heroes, Attenborough was also influenced by the arguments of Alfred Russel Wallace. Known as the 'forgotten hero' who co-discovered evolution, the naturalist was honoured when a statue was unveiled at the Natural History Museum by Sir David in 2013, on the hundredth anniversary of Wallace's death.

'For me, there is no more admirable character in the history of science,' said Attenborough of Wallace.

*

Being a child in the 1920s and 1930s was a very different experience to childhood in the 21st century, as Attenborough has often reflected. Parents are so much more protective of their children now and there is a culture of 'health and safety' that was not so prevalent then.

'When I was a boy, I could cycle out of town and be in fields in ten minutes,' he said. 'I knew where the birds' nests and badger setts were.' For instance, he remembered how, when he was 'about 13', he cycled from Leicester to the Lake District and back again, collecting fossils and staying in youth hostels. 'I was away for three weeks, and my mother and father didn't know where I was,' he said. 'I doubt many parents would let children do that now.'

*

However, a more safety-conscious culture comes with many advantages, and childhood accidents were commonplace in the early decades of the 20th century. He said the closest he has come to death was when he fell 37m (120ft) from a cliff in the Lake District. 'I was climbing the cliff, or thought I was!' he said. This was prior to his television career, he explained. 'It was when I was young and foolish.'

*

However, he would not swap the chance to have roamed free as a child for anything. When he was asked if there was something he experienced as a child that he would wish that teenagers could do today, his answer was simple: 'Getting lost.'

*

During his teenage years, his father introduced him to Jacquetta Hawkes, the daughter of an eminent scientist and herself a prominent archaeologist. It was a pivotal meeting that played a big part in verifying his interest in becoming a naturalist. 'When she showed interest in my fossils I felt I was walking 18 inches off the ground, and two weeks later a big parcel arrived,' he remembered.

'In those days you only had parcels on your birthday or Christmas and this wasn't either, so I was unbelievably excited,' he said. Inside, there were 'some amazing treasures', including a 'dried sea horse, a piece of Roman pottery, an Anglo-Saxon coin . . . She wrote that she hoped I'd like to add them to my collection. Well, can you imagine . . .'

*

Another distinguished early influence was Archibald Belaney, a British conservationist better known as Grey Owl. Together with Richard, David attended a lecture by Grey Owl, at De Montfort Hall, Leicester.

Richard remembered that David was 'bowled over by the man's determination to save the beaver, by his profound knowledge of the flora and fauna of the Canadian wilderness and by his warnings of ecological disaster should the delicate balance between them be destroyed'.

He added that 'the idea that mankind was endangering nature by recklessly despoiling and plundering its riches was unheard of at the time, but it is one that has remained part of Dave's own credo to this day'.

It also had an influence on Richard: in 1999 he directed a film about Belaney, called *Grey Owl*, starring Pierce Brosnan in the title role.

*

David Attenborough has retained his sense of childlike wonder through the years. Although he has devoted his life to exploring the planet, he wishes he had explored less of it than he has. 'I wish the world was twice as big – and half of it was still unexplored,' he once explained.

School days

David was sent to a local school in Leicester, Wyggeston Grammar School for Boys. His parents did not believe in sending their children off to boarding school, something so many households did at the time. Instead, they preferred to keep their beloved offspring closer to home.

'My parents were great supporters of grammar – as opposed to boarding – schools and took the view that they had not brought a child into the world to send him off into the care of strangers,' he said.

*

DID YOU KNOW?

In 2015, Attenborough opened a school building known as the Attenborough Building in Richmond-upon-Thames. It was built for the school's sixth-formers, who were thrilled by his visit on the opening day.

*

Fittingly, given the educational blood that runs through his veins, Attenborough is full of admiration for those who taught him as a child. He was at school during the early years of World War II, which meant 'everyone of military age was in the services, so most of the teachers were elderly', he said.

'I was astonished even then how much time all the teachers devoted to us kids, giving up their evenings to help us,' he reflected.

*

He also has a lot of time for the teachers of today. In 2019, he praised the teachers of the 21st century for the leading role they have played on the issue of single-use plastic.

'Primary school teachers have got hold of this and they have instructed their classes,' he said. 'I get 30 letters a day, of which a high proportion are from children. They've learned about it at school. So thank you, primary school teachers, for what they're doing.'

*

Many people of his generation despair of younger people but Attenborough does not. He believes that the younger generation are more concerned about the future of the planet – and not just out of self-interest. 'Young people – they care,' he said. 'They know that this is the world that they're going to grow up in, that they're going to spend the rest of their lives in. But, I think it's more idealistic than that. They actually believe that humanity, human species, has no right to destroy and despoil regardless.'

*

However, his early years at Wyggeston Grammar were not always smooth for Attenborough, whose school reports would sometimes make such observations as: 'Good work, spoilt by silly behaviour.'

He has admitted that he found some subjects pointless. 'There was so much rote learning; I can still say, "Amo, amas, amat, amamus, amatis, amant", but God knows what that has done for me,' he said. 'I wasn't interested in most of the subjects we had to study. I defy anybody to be interested in Latin declensions or French irregular verbs.'

*

But when he reached sixth form, a new teacher entered his life, and positively kindled Attenborough's passion for learning.

The teacher, Horace Lacey, taught Attenborough biology 'with gusto', he said. Lacey was 'a stocky man who walked like a gamecock with his head turned to one side, and he had wiry, frizzy hair'. Lacey's enthusiasm for his subject 'spilled over', said Attenborough.

Indeed, although Attenborough admitted to being 'not in the least interested in steam engines', he was taken in by Lacey's stories about Sir Nigel Gresley, the engineer who designed and built locomotives for the Great Western Railway/London and North Eastern Railway. His teacher's 'sheer infectious enthusiasm made me seem delighted by it all', remembered the former pupil.

When Lacey retired, Attenborough, who was by now famous, was invited to the school prize day. 'It was my first opportunity to say thank you to him,' he remembered. 'I started off on a eulogy of dear old Horace, going on about how good he was, but was suddenly completely thrown when I glanced toward him across the school hall and saw he was so moved that his shoulders were wracked with sobs.'

*

The school used streaming, which separated pupils based on their intelligence. Attenborough described this system without any sentiment.

'If you were extremely bright, you took classics; if you were extremely thick, you did woodwork,' he said. 'In between was science, then modern languages. I was in the science stream.'

★

Another teacher who was particularly influential taught Attenborough after school. Frederick, Attenborough's father, discovered that one of the masters at University College, Leicester, where Frederick was the principal, had previously studied geology at university. He proved to have an important role in the life of the future national treasure.

'His name was J R Cottrill and he was teaching physics at the time, but he saw me after school and guided my interest and advised me which books to read, which was very helpful,' said Attenborough.

The school had 'a good amateur dramatic society' in which he was involved, 'though not to the degree that my brother Richard was', said David. 'We did a lot of Gilbert and Sullivan,' he said. 'I can still sing the whole of the first act of *HMS Pinafore*, playing all the parts, without pausing for breath.'

★

As the brothers grew up, moments of mischief between them were far from unheard of. For instance, Richard once locked David in a padded cell in the former Leicestershire and Rutland County Lunatic Asylum, now part of the University of Leicester's campus and called the Fielding Johnson Building.

★

DID YOU KNOW?

When the Welsh island of Skomer featured on Attenborough's *Wild Isles* series in 2023, the broadcast led to a surge in visitor numbers. 'It's great that the series is making more people realize that we have really amazing wildlife right here,' said a thrilled local warden.

In 1941, Attenborough's father received three geological specimens: one of shale and two of quartz. In a letter of thanks to their sender, Lieutenant Colonel Neame of Collycroft House, Frederick revealed that he'd passed them on to his son, David.

'I cannot tell you just where they have come from and I doubt whether it is possible to do so since they are specimens of rocks which are fairly widely distributed,' he wrote. 'My son, however, is very glad to have them; he has labelled them and added them to his collection.'

*

A year later, Frederick wrote to the Secretaries of the Geological Society of London concerning an education scheme he'd been told about. Again, David loomed large in his missive. 'I am personally interested because my son, who is now sixteen, hopes to become a Geologist,' he said.

*

Attenborough might have something of a saintly reputation now but he has admitted to being a little cheeky as a child. He even cut some corners at school.

For instance, during a visit to Bradgate Park in Leicester, he confessed to cheating to get top marks in a biology exam, and helping his classmates to do the same. It all started with a stroke of luck when a caretaker left a tin marked 'zoology practical' on a desk.

Attenborough seized the chance to discover what the exam would be about. 'I picked it up and shook it. It rattled so I knew it was crayfish,' he said. 'I knew where I could get crayfish – the stream at Bradgate Park, so I headed there. I told all the other boys.'

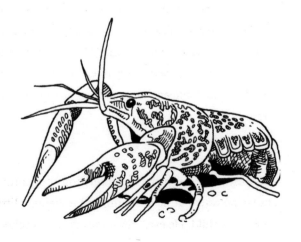

This gave the whole class the chance to practise on crayfish and they got distinctions in the exam. Attenborough remembered how their teacher was quite overwhelmed and told the boys: 'You are the most brilliant class I've ever had.'

*

Another of Frederick's letters shows that he withheld consent for his son to enrol in the AA Battery of the Home Guard during World War II, as he felt David might be moving in a different direction. 'I regret that I must withhold consent for my son D. F. Attenborough to enrol,' wrote the father in 1944, because 'he is to take the Higher Schools Certificate Examination shortly and his future plans are uncertain.'

*

DID YOU KNOW?

RRS *Sir David Attenborough*, a polar research vessel owned by the Natural Environment Research Council and operated by the British Antarctic Survey for the purposes of both research and logistic support, was named after him. She began her sea trials on 21 October 2020. The ship is about 125m (410ft) long, with a beam of about 24m (79ft). The draught is about 7m (23ft) with a planned cruising speed of 13 knots (24kph or 15mph) and a range of 19,000 nautical miles (35,000km or 22,000 miles) at that speed.

*

Attenborough has built a gloriously mixed fan base. Who else is admired across so many generations? For the man himself, this is because the very topic he is dealing in is one of inevitable universal concern. 'My stock-in-trade is appreciated by kids of seven and professors of seventy and everything in between,' he has said.

*

Sir David has shown great compassion for animals and that compassionate streak was something he inherited from his mother and father.

Frederick and Mary organized committees to care for child refugees from the Spanish Civil War and Nazi Germany, and they also took into the family two Jewish refugee children, Helga and Irene Bejach, who remained as the boys' adopted sisters for eight years.

'It is just an indication of what his parents were like and a lot of that has rubbed off on him,' said his cameraman, Gavin Thurston. 'If I could take anything away from my time with David it would be how you treat people, and that trickles down to how you treat animals or nature.'

*

Another refugee, Marianne, who was 12, the same age as David, gave him a piece of amber containing prehistoric creatures. She had been given it by her father, to pass on to whoever would be looking after her. It was a remarkably prescient offering.

'It felt surprisingly warm and light in my hand, but what made me fall in love with amber was what I discovered inside it,' remembered David. 'I found something miraculous,' he said. 'There were insects preserved in astonishing detail.'

On another occasion, speaking about a different piece of amber, in which a bee was encapsulated, he commented that it was 'hard to imagine a more perfect time capsule than this' because 'this little bee has been trapped in there for, literally, millions of years'.

*

Having grown up fascinated by and immersed in nature, Attenborough feels that the children of today are increasingly disconnected from the natural world.

'If it's not health and safety telling you you've got to wear a gas mask,' he told an interviewer, 'it's somebody telling you it's illegal to pick up a bird's feather. It's certainly illegal to peer into a nest,' he added.

While accepting there were concerns over welfare, he felt 'the interaction between humans and the natural world has been constrained, and that is a human loss' that 'could ultimately be a loss to the natural world because people won't understand it any more'.

2

Hitting the Small Screen

University and beyond

In 1950, David married Jane Elizabeth Ebsworth Oriel.
She was originally from Merthyr Tydfil, a small Welsh
town 32km (20 miles) or so north of the capital, Cardiff.
They were 24 and 23 respectively, and they moved
into a home together in Richmond-upon-Thames in
London.

Nearby was the beauty of Richmond Park. The largest
of London's Royal Parks, it was created as a deer park
by Charles I in the early 17th century and has become
of national and international importance for wildlife
conservation.

The Friends of Richmond Park, a charitable organization, has 3,800 members, and boasts Sir David Attenborough as one of its patrons.

In 2023, he planted an English Oak tree to officially open a new woodland in Richmond Park as part of The Queen's Green Canopy initiative.

★

At the end of World War II, Attenborough's father had told him that if he 'wanted to go to one of these senior universities' then he had to earn his place by getting a scholarship. 'He said if you want that privilege you've got to earn it and not just by money,' remembered Attenborough.

He 'dutifully got a scholarship' by taking a paper in geology, travelling up to Nottingham University and 'as it were eavesdropping' on first-year geological students as part of his research beforehand. His reward was a place at Cambridge University.

*

DID YOU KNOW?

The trait David most dislikes in others is falsehood and the thing that makes him most unhappy is conflict.

Moving on to Cambridge University, he said that science courses 'didn't cut too many corners' and the workload was so heavy that those taking them 'had to work in vacations'.

'If you read science, you didn't laze around on the river with girls – like people reading English and philosophy – but it was a paradisiacal time,' he said. 'I got a 2.1 in natural sciences' but he expressed concern that a particular topic brought his overall score down: 'I found the three-dimensional crystallography inscrutable and I'm sure it let me down.'

*

At Cambridge, he came across a club that appealed to his sense of adventure. Founded in 1904, the Cambridge University Expeditions Society is the oldest expeditions society in the world. As well as Attenborough, its glittering alumni include the ornithologist Sir Peter Scott and the scientist–explorer Sir Vivian Fuchs.

*

After university, from 1947, he spent two years in the Royal Navy, stationed in North Wales and Scotland. He had hoped it would be an opportunity to see the world, particularly after he met old naval hands who talked about a potential destination in what was then Ceylon (now Sri Lanka). But instead he was sent to be part of the Reserve Fleet in the Firth of Forth in Scotland.

After his naval years, the possibility of returning to education did not appeal to David. 'I thought I cannot go back to being a student and I got a job,' he said. He was now a married man and didn't want his wife and himself to have to survive on a measly student grant.

The working man

Not that being a working man was an immediate joy for him. Attenborough has been lucky enough to spend decades working in a job he loves and being paid to follow his passion. It wasn't always the case, though. Asked what was the worst job he had ever had, he remembered, 'working in a factory during the war, making plastic buttons'.

*

After university and the war, he got a job in publishing, where he was able to work on manuscripts about very 'Attenboroughian' topics, including tadpoles. He was the most junior and the most recently recruited member of the team. The runt of the litter.

'My job there was footling really, but perfectly OK, the right way to start, the equivalent of making the tea, it was crossing commas out or occasionally on a good day putting one in, if you felt pretty bold.'

He has remembered eating his lunch, usually a sandwich, in a garden on a bomb site, opposite the office. He would check proofs of the books, which he found moderately interesting, but also not the sort of work he wanted to do, after working so hard for his university degree.

He would keep checking the clock, to see if more time had passed, but the clock moved agonizingly slowly. He said this 'dismal' revelation 'depressed' him. He eventually got so frustrated by the slow movement of the clock that he turned his desk around to face a blank wall, rather than the snail-like clock.

'And it was then,' he wrote in his memoir *Life on Air*, 'that I decided that this was not the way I wanted to spend the rest of my life. Maybe my future was not, after all, to be a gentleman publisher.'

The book world's loss was to be television's gain.

★

It is not surprising that the man with itchy feet and a passion for the outdoors eventually found the book publishing process 'inexpressibly boring because it took so long'.

By this time, he was buying *The Times* newspaper daily. As an 'embryonic city gent', he confided in *Life on Air*, he felt he 'had to' be seen with a copy in the office, and he would 'occasionally' even read it.

One of his favourite sections was the jobs page. So when he saw a job advert for a radio producer, he was tempted to apply. Having failed to land himself a job that involved roaming around the planet, he thought the radio role might at least allow him to talk to such people and enjoy the experience vicariously.

His impatient nature was nagging at him. 'It's the same kind of thing as thinking up ideas for books only it's probably quicker,' he said. 'I don't see why I shouldn't be able to do that, I mean it might be quite interesting.'

*

He was rejected for that job but was later phoned, at work, by a woman from BBC television, who had seen his application for the radio job. The call caused him some discomfort. He said getting such a call at work 'absolutely horrified' him and he felt like 'crouching underneath the desk, saying not so loud'.

'I thought it was absolutely scandalous that anyone should ring me up on the office phone and have the effrontery to suggest that I might leave the firm, the very firm whose chair I was sitting on, whose phone I was using.'

The woman told him the contract would be for around three to six months' work, which put him off the idea. Television was a new medium at the time and no one could be sure it was going to be a steady or long-term career path. He told her: 'I'm a married man, I have a son, I can't go on some flibbertygibbit enterprise like that.'

*

However, he eventually decided to take the job, and he remembers well the day that he finally left the publisher's office and the feeling of relief he enjoyed. It was a Friday in September 1952, when he 'finally abandoned' the desk at which he'd been so bored.

Big break at the BBC

His next challenge was a training day. It was held in an office block near the Marylebone Road. He and around a dozen other hopefuls filed in. Most were hoping to join the theatrical or musical wings of the BBC – only Attenborough and one other wanted to join the Talks department.

A man delivered a lecture, attempting to explain the structure of the BBC by chalking a series of rectangles on a blackboard, which he connected with lines, some of them straight lines, some of them dotted. It came as 'no surprise' to Attenborough when he realized the man was 'the author of an authoritative book on witchcraft in medieval England'.

This set the tone for two weeks of lectures, to try to teach the hopefuls all they needed to know about the BBC. After that, Attenborough went to Alexandra Palace to meet the Talks department team.

He has written that they had 'no identifiable qualifications for their jobs'. He recalled a 'large and effusive Dutchman', a 'promising painter' and a 'small, vivacious bird-like lady' with 'rather more of the eagle than the wren'. In another withering verdict, he said the team was marshalled by a man whose 'primary qualification' was being 'an expert on the Icelandic sagas'.

However, for the three months of training he got paid what he would have been paid for a year's work back in his publishing job. He estimates his pay for the 12 weeks would have been around £1,100. This is approximately £40,000 in today's money.

*

DID YOU KNOW?

When he joined the BBC as a trainee in 1952, Attenborough had only ever watched one television programme.

Broadcasting was certainly an entirely different beast when Attenborough decided to join the industry. In 2023, 480 TV channels were available in the UK alone. Back in the early 1950s, there was just one: the BBC. It was only broadcast in two cities – Birmingham and London – and nearly all transmissions went out live.

Indeed, thanks to World War II, during which the BBC suspended transmissions, TV in Britain had only been running for ten years when he joined up. The televising of the 1953 Coronation, which truly put television on the British map for the first time, was just months away.

★

One of Attenborough's earliest television appearances came when a team needed an example of a Caucasian man and he was chosen to appear live on air. He was not required to say anything but appeared, in profile, on the screen.

★

When Attenborough started in television, there had already been two main series covering animals. The superintendent of London Zoo, George Cansdale, fronted series including *Heads, Tails and Feet*, *Looking at Animals* and *All About Animals*, which made him a household name.

He took animals from London Zoo to the BBC's studios in Alexandra Palace and examined them on a table covered with a doormat. Occasionally, as Attenborough recalls with vim in his book *Adventures of a Young Naturalist*, things would go wrong, and the animals would relieve themselves over the mat or over Cansdale himself. Some of them bit him. On other occasions, the animals would run off, and once an African squirrel hid in the studio's ventilation system for several days.

Other animal output came courtesy of the Belgian broadcaster Armand Denis and his wife, the British-born wildlife documentary film maker and presenter, Michaela Denis. Their debut effort for the BBC included footage of giraffes, lions and elephants in their natural habitat of Africa. This offered many viewers their first opportunity to see such magnificent beasts in motion. Their series, *On Safari*, proved very popular among British viewers and the couple are credited with both revolutionizing wildlife documentaries on television and blazing a trail for Attenborough to follow.

*

Attenborough saw strengths and weaknesses in the efforts of the Denises and Cansdale. The strength of the Denises' programme was the opportunity to see animals roam freely in their natural terrain, rather than the jarring surroundings of a television studio. However, the latter offered unpredictability and suspense.

Just 26 years of age, Attenborough started to devise in his head a programme that would wed the strengths of both of these formats. His early times in television had seen him employed as a 'jobbing producer', he wrote, working on 'music recitals, archaeological quizzes, political discussions and ballet performances'.

*

Meanwhile, his move from publishing to broadcasting had been an eye-opening experience for Attenborough.

On his first day in television, he was absolutely flabbergasted by the condition of the workplace, which was not at all what he had expected. He turned up to 'extraordinary studios, which looked to me like a junk shop really. I mean piles of furniture, I mean you edged your way through this junk yard and in the middle, boiling hot lights, there's this tiny pool of light, intense light where all these things are happening.'

*

Having been thrown in at the deep end, he did his first shifts as a television employee. He remembers how gruelling he found the experience at first. By the end of the evening he was, he said, 'emotionally [w]rung out. It was the middle of the night and one thing and another, all I want[ed] to do was have a drink really.'

However, after the drink, he was given a lesson in professionalism by his boss, Paul Johnstone. 'Paul went back to his office to my surprise and sat down at the desk with a Quarto notebook.' And this was his 'faults book', remembered Attenborough. He 'went through and he wrote down all the things he thought he had done wrong in the programme'.

*

Overseas trips were far less common in broadcasting in the 1950s compared with today. After he joined the corporation in 1952 it was 'internal BBC politics' that led Attenborough to focus on documenting nature overseas rather than in Britain.

He made an agreement with the BBC to focus on global wildlife while the corporation's Natural History Unit, founded in Bristol in 1957, would produce nature shows set in Britain.

'There was a chap trying to establish Bristol then as a centre of natural history. He knew which strings to pull and I could see things coming to a head,' he said.

'Eventually we had a meeting and it was agreed I wouldn't look at British natural history at all. Instead, I would go to Africa, South America and so on, and [they] could deal with natural history in Britain,' he said, in 2023. 'I stuck to that until very recently.'

★

DID YOU KNOW?

Attenborough is very much not a fan of flying. 'I loathe getting on an airplane,' he said. He isn't fond of airports, either, though he accepts that they are necessary for his travel bug. 'I always think when I go in there and see this seething mass of humanity queuing, that once I'm at my destination it's going to get better. And it does.'

Attenborough the producer

A short film, *Coelacanth*, which featured biologist Julian Huxley discussing the rediscovery of the coelacanth, was Attenborough's first television credit as a producer.

The coelacanth is a primitive bony fish thought to have been a vital precursor to all backboned animals that ventured onto land. The primitive-looking fish was believed for a long time to have gone extinct along with the dinosaurs 65 million years ago. However, in 1938, it was rediscovered by a South African museum curator on a local fishing trawler, paving the way for Attenborough's programme.

It was an 'exciting scientific discovery', said Attenborough, a 'living fossil whose entrails were likely to reveal new evidence about evolutionary history'. It was also exciting for his career, when the BBC ordered a ten-minute programme to be made as soon as possible.

Attenborough was asked to use his own grounding in biology to convince Huxley to front the programme. He did so and when Huxley arrived at the studio, the young producer had filled a bath in the dressing room with pickled sharks, codfish and salamanders.

The preparation for the show was loose and brief. There was no script and teleprompters were yet to be invented, so all they could do was agree on the rough approach that Huxley intended to follow. Then Attenborough sat in the control gallery and hoped that the presenter would do well. With no guide on what sequence Huxley would follow, Attenborough cut between shots of pickled fish and photographs of a freshly caught coelacanth.

He said it was quite a 'relief' when his boss seemed pleased with the show. It marked the end of his first 12-week term as a trainee and he had done enough in those three months to be offered his first staff job, as an assistant producer.

★

The first programme Attenborough made was watched by barely ten thousand people. How things have changed. In 2019, his series *Our Planet* became Netflix's most-watched original documentary, viewed by 33 million people in its first month alone.

★

Attenborough has said that the Talks department of the BBC covered anything that was 'non-fiction' – often topics that had not been shown on television before – and that the team found themselves developing a new visual grammar to present this original material.

They were experimenting: the sorts of suggestion they talked over were putting a mirror on the ceiling of the studio and filming from there, or ways to mix live and archive footage most honestly. Sometimes, during a live broadcast, a camera would break down. On one occasion, all the cameras broke down. 'The days of the finger-snapping whiz-kid director with hair-trigger reactions were still some time off – but we did our best,' Attenborough said. Indeed, he added, sometimes the director would run off, saying they could not take the pressure of live broadcasting any longer.

★

One of Attenborough's earliest collaborations as a young TV producer was a musical one, with Alan Lomax, the American music expert. Lomax spent almost seven decades as a folklorist and ethnographer, collecting, archiving and analysing folk songs and music in America. He had a 'wide smile' and a 'Texan drawl', remembered Attenborough.

He was a good match for Attenborough. 'I had become interested in folk music through the Third Programme, now Radio 3,' said David. When he heard Lomax was in the UK, making shows about flamenco, a light bulb of inspiration went off in his head. 'When I heard them, I thought it would be a good idea to make a series about traditional music here,' he said.

'Alan was very enthusiastic and soon musicians from all over Britain and Ireland were coming to the studios at Alexandra Palace to take part in our series called *Song Hunter*.'

Among the guests was Margaret Barry, the Irish Traveller, traditional singer and banjo player. Her performance did not go smoothly, and not only because she had left her false teeth behind in the dressing room. 'She left her banjo under the studio lights, so when she came to sing "She Moved Through the Fair" not a string was in tune, and she had taken her teeth out,' Attenborough recalled. 'The audience disagreed, but I thought she was magnificent.'

*

One day, early in his time with the BBC, Attenborough filled in for an interviewer but his performance did not immediately impress his bosses, as he discovered many years later.

The interview had been with Gordon Pirie, an Olympic long-distance runner. After having his face caked with make-up, Attenborough sat down under the strong studio lights to interview the runner. He was told that, in order to make the shot work, he would have to look not directly at his interviewee, but a short distance away.

Both men found this ruling off-putting as the red light came on the camera, to indicate that it was time for the interview to begin. Pirie gave incredibly curt answers to the questions he was asked and Attenborough began to insert into his own questions the information he wanted the runner to give, which only made the exchange more uneven.

When he asked Pirie if it were true that he trained in hobnailed boots, the runner agreed that he did. Attenborough persevered, asking why he did this. 'Cos when I take 'em off, I go faster,' he replied. At this stage, the torturous interview was brought to a close.

Attenborough's loyal and kind wife, Jane, told him he had done well, but it was not until decades later that he got his eyes on a memo that gave the BBC's official verdict. It read: 'Attenborough is an intelligent young man and I'm delighted to have him as a trainee producer but he should not be used as an interviewer again because his teeth are too big.'

Sir David has hardly been off our screens since. This story could encourage us all to not give up our dreams at the first setback.

★

The BBC was known widely as 'Auntie' back in the 1950s but this was not a term that Attenborough and his colleagues ever used. Instead, they called it the 'Beeb' or the 'Corporation'. Nevertheless, he thought Auntie was a fitting name. 'If Auntie did exist, she lived in Broadcasting House.'

★

He has compared the evening broadcasting schedule of the BBC in those days to how a 'very good hostess' might 'arrange an evening meal', with an 'hors d'oeuvre', a 'main course' and 'something less challenging'. Although the male announcer for the evening would usually be wearing a dinner jacket and black tie, beneath his desk he might have secretly been wearing 'a pair of old slacks'.

★

One of Attenborough's early shows was called *Animal Patterns*. This one was also tied in with a zoo. The three-part series saw him and the naturalist Julian Huxley bring to the studio a variety of animals from London Zoo, to help explain the diversity of animal colours and markings.

They also discussed a wide variety of other aspects of animal life, including their use of camouflage, warning signals and courtship displays.

★

While filming *Animal Patterns* in 1953, Attenborough met and become friends with Jack Lester, the curator of the reptile house at London Zoo. Lester invited him to come along and film an expedition he was planning to Sierra Leone. The curator wanted to capture snakes for the zoo, and also snatch a white-necked rockfowl (*Picathartes gymnocephalus*), which had never been kept in a European zoo before.

Attenborough jumped at the chance. He was keen to film on location and he immediately sensed that

Lester's quest to find the bird would make a dramatic and compelling storyline for television viewers to follow. How right he was.

In front of the camera

Zoo Quest was the first major television series to feature David Attenborough, who had been pivotal in getting the series commissioned in the first place. He decided to arrange a lunch, where bosses from the BBC and London Zoo could meet, with the impression that the other side already had the programme in mind.

The lunch took place at the zoo's restaurant and, by the end, each side believed that it was in their interests to join the plans the other side had. The following day, the show was commissioned, to the 'incredulous delight' of Attenborough, he recalled.

In each series, Attenborough travelled with staff from London Zoo to a tropical country to capture an animal for the zoo's collection. At the end of the series, the animals the team had captured were introduced in the studio, where experts from the zoo discussed them. It would run over seven series with 42 episodes in total.

*

Zoo Quest debuted on 21 December 1954. Attenborough travelled, as a producer, to Sierra Leone with zoologists Jack Lester and Alfred Woods, to document them collecting animals for London Zoo.

Attenborough got his chance to present the series quite by chance. Plan A was for Jack Lester to present the studio portion of the programme, while Attenborough worked as producer. But then Lester developed a mysterious tropical disease soon after returning from Africa, and was able to present only one section before he was hospitalized. However, the programme had already been scheduled so there was no time to look further afield for a fresh presenter. Instead, Attenborough took over the presenter's role.

He was the first person to film many rare and elusive species, such as the Komodo dragon. Collecting animals for the zoo from the wild does not sit well with modern attitudes to animal welfare and Sir David would not repeat the practice now.

★

Attenborough enjoyed his trip to Sierra Leone, the first country he visited for *Zoo Quest*, where he recorded drumming and playing a type of wooden xylophone known as a balangi. Recording music on his travels would become quite a theme for Attenborough, as we shall see.

After its debut in 1954, the series steadily gained viewers as each episode went out. For the first time in his life, Attenborough was recognized and stopped in the street. He would get used to this as the years and decades rolled by but it was at first a very novel experience.

★

During the quest for the rare *Picathartes gymnocephalus*, they had a similar encounter. They were three months into filming, still trying to find the bird – to the point that David noted in the first episode, 'You wouldn't see the damn thing, but at the end you'd say: "So we continued our quest for the Picathartes . . ."'

When Attenborough and his cameraman were driving down London's Oxford Street one day, a bus driver leaned out of his bus and shouted: ''Ello Dave, are we or are we not going to find pica-bloody-thartes?'

★

As a rising star in broadcasting, Attenborough was soon rubbing shoulders with powerful people, and one of his earliest jobs was to produce Prime Minister Sir Anthony Eden's Suez broadcast for the nation.

After the nationalization of the Suez Canal by the Egyptian leader, Colonel Abdul Nasser, Eden teamed up with Israel and France to try to retake the canal. The invasion did not go to plan and, following widespread condemnation, Eden was eventually forced to retreat.

So the stakes were high when he approached Attenborough. 'I felt history throbbing around me and I felt I had some sense of urgency and mission,' he said, remembering how Eden, who was sick in bed, asked his advice for the wording of his speech.

'"Shall I address the people as 'friends'?" Eden asked me. "What do you think?"' Attenborough found this 'extraordinary' and said: 'It became clear to me that he was in no condition to do anything, let alone take a decision as to whether we were going to go to war.'

'Eventually I think I said: "Perhaps, Prime Minister, you should get some rest."'

★

Zoo Quest was ground-breaking for its time, as it was among the first natural history programmes to film animals in their natural habitats rather than in a studio.

Sir David reflected that animal programmes used to be entirely filmed in a studio and 'consisted of an expert from London Zoo who brought animals from Regent's Park and exhibited them live in the studio, usually on a table covered by a doormat'.

'He talked about them while they struggled to escape from the glare of the studio lights, occasionally wet down his front, bit him – or even escaped,' he said.

*

While there was a sense of expedition to *Zoo Quest*, Attenborough is keen to distance the series' approach from adventure shows of today.

'They are deliberately programmes where someone who the audience can identify with will be meeting snakes or whatever it is, which is a slightly different type of programme,' he said. In this kind of show, Attenborough said, natural history is the 'supporting cast'. He continued: 'I'd done adventure programmes back in the '50s. But in more recent years I've tried to do programmes where natural history is the star.'

Not that he thinks adventure shows are invalid. 'There's a place for all the programmes, such as crocodile hunting with the late Steve Irwin, or *Deadly 60* with Steve Backshall,' he said, because 'very often people will be drawn to a programme because it's a "Boys' Own" adventure, discover that natural history in itself is rather interesting and will try other programmes.'

★

The photographer working on *Zoo Quest* was a Czech cameraman called Charles Lagus. He had the honour of being the first cameraman engaged by the BBC to shoot natural history footage. He later worked in Australia on Peter Scott's *Faraway Look* in 1957 and on a host of other UK series, including Anglia Television's *Lure of the Dolphin* in 1976, the BBC's *Animal Magic* and ITV's *Nature Watch*.

Writing in his *Adventures of a Young Naturalist*, Attenborough recalled his first meeting with Lagus, when he convinced him to join the team. 'We drank a little beer,' he remembered fondly, and 'laughed at the same jokes'. It only took Lagus two drinks to agree to sign up.

Another to join the crew was Alf Woods, whom Attenborough remembered as a 'wily and sagacious' zoo keeper. Woods took care of the animals after they were caught.

★

There was a stand-off between the team and the BBC management over which type of film they would use to record the footage in *Zoo Quest*. The team wanted to film their trips on 16mm film instead of the 35mm film that was then the corporation's standard. The team won and this meant the series was filmed on colour stock, as it offered better quality. However, the BBC did not begin colour broadcasting until the late 1960s.

When footage of series one of *Zoo Quest* was unearthed by the BBC in 2016, Sir David said he was 'astonished' to discover that the series had been shot in colour. 'It's impossible, we shot in black and white,' he said.

Lagus said admiringly of the footage: 'At its best it's as good as any colour you see now, quite staggering for the period that it was filmed in.'

*

Although the first series was entitled simply *Zoo Quest*, the subsequent series all had more specific titles:

Zoo Quest to Guiana (1955)

Zoo Quest to West Africa (1955)

Zoo Quest for a Dragon (1956)

Zoo Quest for the Paradise Birds (1957)

Zoo Quest in Paraguay (1959)

Zoo Quest to Madagascar (1961)

Quest Under Capricorn (1963)

*

He may be a nature lover, but Sir David is terrified of rats.

It might surprise some people that Attenborough, who has encountered all manner of life on Earth, would be scared of any creature, but it's true. 'I really, really hate rats,' he said in 2011, on BBC Radio 4.

'I've handled deadly spiders, snakes and scorpions without batting an eyelid, but if I see a rat I'll be the first to run,' he said. 'If a rat appears in a room, I have to work hard to prevent myself from jumping on the nearest table!'

Fear of rats is known as musophobia. For Attenborough, it started when he was staying in a thatched hut in a village in the Solomon Islands. 'I was out there filming, when a thunderstorm broke out one night,' he remembered. As he tried to get to sleep, he felt a movement on the sheet around his feet. 'I flicked on my torch and there was a rat running across me,' he said. 'I looked around. There were rats everywhere . . . Needless to say, I abandoned the hut.'

He also had an unpleasant rodent run-in while filming at a temple in India. When he returned early to the lodge one night, he sat on the toilet and a rat leapt up from between his thighs, ran off and hid under his bed.

He said that, when you are 'out in the bush, animals are frightened of you and if things get rough, you can always do something to scare them off'. But 'the thing about rats is that they are not scared off and they actually invade the area where you think you are boss,' he said. 'On top of that, they are associated with disease and filth. They do, after all, live in sewers.'

However, he says he believes that his 'irrational horror of them' stems from the fact that 'they live at such close quarters with us' and 'while they sensibly keep out of the way when they can, they don't have any real fear of us'.

Collector of sounds

A little-known fact about Attenborough is that he was something of a pioneer in bringing world music to the UK. Indeed, although he has had the chance to watch again old shows he made decades ago, Attenborough does not find that as evocative an experience as listening to music from the time.

'Music takes me back to those places 50 or 60 years ago,' he said, but 'visual images don't.' In fact, as well as gathering animals during his years making *Zoo Quest*, he also spent time gathering music. 'In the day we filmed the man from the zoo pouncing on pythons,' he said, 'but in the evenings I recorded music.'

When he returned from the trips, he handed the recordings to the BBC Sound Library. In 2018, a journalist went for a rustle through the library to see what he could find from the Attenborough depositions. He found more than 60 music items, from West Africa, Latin America, Indonesia, the South Pacific, Madagascar and Australia, credited to David Attenborough as collector.

On Christmas Day 2018, he presented a radio programme revisiting the recordings, which nobody, including him, had heard for years. 'These tracks remind me of the musicians who, half a century ago, shared with me their fascinating and wonderful music,' he said.

*

So many musicians did just that. In 1957, when he travelled through Java and Bali on his way to film on the island of Komodo, he discovered gamelan music, the traditional ensemble music of the Javanese, Sundanese and Balinese peoples of Indonesia, made up principally of percussion instruments. He quickly fell in love with the sound of it all.

'Bali then was almost unaffected by outside influence,' he said. 'Every village had its gamelan, 20 or more players. They practised almost every night. None of the music was written and the master taught each player his part individually. Then they played together with extraordinary precision and verve.'

Two years later, *Zoo Quest* took Attenborough to Paraguay, where he discovered the country's traditional harp music. 'I recorded a group with two harps and three guitars, including a huge bass instrument called a guitarrón,' he said. The guitarrón is a large, deep-bodied Mexican six-string acoustic bass.

'We used some of it to accompany images of armadillos trotting over the Chacos desert. One tune, "Pájaro Campana (The Bell Bird)", became the signature tune for the series and Paraguayan harp music became very

popular. When Trío Los Paraguayos came to Britain they were very pleased to find an audience already prepared for their music.' Attenborough is rightly lauded for his mammoth contribution to understanding nature and the environment, but he has helped people understand the world of music, too.

★

When he appeared on the BBC Radio 4 programme *Desert Island Discs* in 2012, Sir David's choices were:

Francisco Yglesia. 'Pájaro Campana' ('The Bell Bird')

Franz Schubert. *Impromptu* No. 1 in F minor

George Frideric Handel. 'And the Glory of the Lord' from the *Messiah*

'Lyre Bird' from *The Life of Birds*

Johann Sebastian Bach. *Goldberg Variations* No. 3

The Gamelan Orchestra. Legong dance

Carl Michael Ziehrer. *Wiener Bürger* ('Waltz of Viennese Citizens')

Wolfgang Amadeus Mozart. 'Soave sia il vento' from *Così Fan Tutte*

His book choice was *Shifts and Expedients of Camp Life* by W B Lord, and his luxury choice was a piano.

In fact, Attenborough has appeared on the show four times in total, having been the 'castaway' guest in 1957, 1979 and 1998 as well as 2012.

In 1957, his luxury was a piano (as in 2012). In 1979, his favourite piece of music was String Quintet No. 4 in G Minor by Mozart, and his luxury was a pair of binoculars. In 1998, his favourite piece of music was

String Quintet in C Major by Schubert, and his luxury was a guitar. His book choice was always the same (but with none chosen in 1957).

He must have made quite an impression: he was later chosen by long-standing presenter Kirsty Young as her favourite-ever *Desert Island Discs* guest.

★

In explaining why music is so important to him, he has charmingly poked fun at himself. 'I see film of myself from then, chasing an anteater, and think "what an odd human being", or "what funny trousers". But hearing the music takes me right back. Sound has that power.'

In 1962, Attenborough filmed in Arnhem Land, Australia. An Aboriginal artist named Magani agreed to show him how bark painting was done. 'I went to his shelter every day to watch him making these extraordinary images of animals, goannas, lizards, kangaroos,' he said, 'but often Magani wasn't there and I was told he had "business", which meant sacred rites.'

Magani let Attenborough attend a coming-of-age ceremony, when boys, painted with lizard figures, slid under a vast didgeridoo. It represented a great serpent, Yurlungur, which was important in their creation myth. 'This marked their coming into maturity,' Attenborough recalled. 'It was a very moving ceremony. All the time the didgeridoo played and this was the voice of Yurlungur. Whenever I hear such music I am transported back to prehistory because the Aboriginal people have lived in Australia for at least 40,000 years. That's way earlier than the cave paintings of Lascaux in France.'

*

Another dalliance with music came when he joined Slash, Shara Nelson and Brian May in a 'pro-badger supergroup' called Artful Badger and Friends to campaign against badger culls.

The group's song, 'Badger Swagger', aimed to help the campaign against the government's plan to kill up to a hundred thousand animals. Rob Cass, the track's creator, said he was thrilled to have 'the wonderful David Attenborough' involved.

Special guests and new friends

During his early years as natural history broadcaster, Attenborough brought home gibbons, chimpanzees, chameleons, snakes, hummingbirds, lemurs and bushbabies. The new guests came with challenges.

'The thing about a bushbaby is that the male establishes its territory by peeing on his hands and putting it all on the walls,' he recalled. 'And after you've had a pair for about six months, you can see people coming into the house, sniffing and going: "Now, that's definitely not mulligatawny soup."'

*

In 2012, he looked back on how much easier it was to make nature documentaries during the 1950s and also how much easier it had been to impress viewers back then.

'You could just turn up and film a Komodo dragon and nobody would have seen one. That was enough,' he said. He could, he added, 'go off with £1,000' and a cameraman to the South Pacific and make a whole show.

★

In 1958, he first met the Queen's children, Charles and Anne, when they toured the BBC's Lime Grove studios. Attenborough introduced them to his pet cockatoo, Cocky. This was the first of many times that his path crossed with the royal family's.

Another of the early shows he was involved in was a game show called *Animal, Vegetable, Mineral?* A panel of experts, including archaeologists, art historians and natural history experts, was asked to identify curious and interesting objects or artifacts from museums and university collections. It ran from 1952 to 1959.

Attenborough was camera director and also the person charged with choosing the artifact for each episode. On one occasion he chose a moustache-lifter used by the Ainu people of Japan, while another time it was the knucklebones of a horse used by the ancient Romans as dice. He wasn't setting out to baffle the experts but to produce an entertaining and interesting television show.

However, the tables were turned for the 1956 Christmas special, when Glyn Daniel and Mortimer Wheeler selected the items to be put to a panel comprising Attenborough and members of the production team. Mortimer was 'undoubtedly' the star of the show, believed Sir David. 'He played outrageously to the gallery, twirling his moustaches, pretending to be initially baffled, then discovering a clue and finally bringing his identification to a triumphant conclusion.'

The recording evenings sound like a lot of fun. The experts and the crew would dine together in the private room of a Kensington restaurant and then jump into taxis which would rush them to Shepherd's Bush and get them on air while the energy and charisma of the dinner were still alive in the group. On one occasion, when the chairman, Glyn Daniel, had had a few too many drinks, this became obvious on air, remembered Attenborough. Journalists who phoned the next day to find out what had happened were told that the lights were particularly strong and hot, and Daniel was suffering from influenza.

*

Another time the press got involved was when guest Julian Huxley insisted that the mystery object was the egg of a reptile, despite Daniel's strong disagreement. Huxley even bet Daniel five pounds that he was right. So, when it was revealed that the item was a snail, Attenborough could not decide whether to focus the camera on the delighted Daniel or the humiliated Huxley. He decided to focus on the egg.

After the show, press photographers arrived to see if they could get a shot of Huxley handing over a five-pound note. 'I didn't think they were likely to get it,' wrote Attenborough, 'and they didn't.'

★

Inevitably, there were moments of confusion on air. When the mystery item was a photograph of the Burning Ghats at Benares (Varanasi), in India, with temples in the background and smoke rising from pyres on which human corpses burned, the scene was very evocative. Two members of the panel couldn't offer even a guess, and the third declared confidently that it was 'the River Thames just above Maidenhead'.

When Attenborough interviewed Konrad Lorenz, the distinguished Austrian zoologist, the expert arrived with a greylag goose. The animal was not delighted to be in a hot, brightly lit television studio. The zoologist had taken the trouble not to be in range of the goose's beak, but the price for this was that he was in range of its other end. The creature duly squirted a jet of green liquid directly over Lorenz.

*

Another mishap came when Attenborough's guest was a rat-catcher called Bill Dalton. He had no end of colourful tales about rodents being discovered in the most unexpected places, including posh hotels. He also often killed rats with a harsh blow from a shovel.

Attenborough told him not to do anything like that on camera and Dalton agreed. However, once they were on air, Dalton grabbed a rat from a cage tightly packed with the creatures. He held it by the tail and whirled it around in the air, explaining that unless he made the rat dizzy, 'the bugger will bite me'. It was, reflected Attenborough, the first time the word had been uttered on British television.

★

Indeed, early reviews for the series were sometimes harsh, remembered producer Paul Johnstone, as critics gave it a 'cold welcome' because 'professors and fossils seemed an unlikely source of entertainment'. Not that all the reviews were harsh. Writing for *The Observer*, the critic C A Lejeune described *Animal, Vegetable, Mineral?* as having 'a sound, full-bodied, vintage flavour'.

Indeed, the series went on to be a success and was credited with an upsurge in interest in archaeology.

A flourishing career

The success of his early shows helped catapult Attenborough up the ladder of broadcasting. On 5 March 1965, *The Times* reported that 'Mr David Attenborough, aged 38' had been appointed to the prestigious new post of controller of BBC2, the channel that had been launched less than a year previously.

It added: 'Mr Attenborough, brother of Richard Attenborough, the actor, is well known to television audiences through his travel and animal programmes, notably his *Zoo Quest* series, which took him all over the world.'

The report noted that Attenborough regarded his new job 'rather dimly' because he was 'not privy' to the ideas of Mike Peacock, the former chief of programmes, BBC2. However, he added, he was 'on the friendliest terms' with Peacock and was sure they could work well together. Attenborough also told reporters that he watched BBC2 frequently and, while he would hesitate to describe it as his favourite channel, it had provided some excellent programmes.

★

Prior to landing the gig, he had been enrolled at the London School of Economics in 1964, studying for a degree in anthropology through a part-time course.

He has admitted he was taken aback by the invitation to be controller of BBC2. He couldn't decide whether to take the job or not. To help him decide, he wrote down a list of advantages and disadvantages. In the end, though, he asked himself, 'Are you a broadcaster or a naturalist? And the answer had to be I was actually a broadcaster.'

He told the BBC he felt 'there was no point in coming to do it for less than three years and I promise you I will do that', but added that he thought there was 'not any chance' he would do it for more than five years.

His appointment to the BBC role was 'greeted with scepticism', said *The Guardian*, and 'he was considered lightweight, a youthful bit of eye-candy'. However, he handsomely proved the doubters wrong.

He felt all along that he had been underestimated. 'Everybody forgot I wasn't just a naturalist – I was always a trained TV man,' he told the *Daily Express* in 1965. 'Hell, I love it. I watch everything. Straight home from the office – switch to BBC Two – see all my babies.'

*

He felt he was in a no-lose situation at the time because BBC2 was 'absolutely at rock bottom and that is the greatest time to go in on anything, when it is at rock bottom, because it can only go up'.

*

He got the first of many feathers in his cap when he commissioned an epic, 12-part series called *Civilisation*, presented by art historian Kenneth Clark. Clark was not sure when first approached whether he wanted to take part. He recalled later that what convinced him was Attenborough's use of the word 'civilisation' to sum up what the series would be about.

Its scope would indeed be very broad. It covered, said a *Guardian* review at the time, 'art and architecture, literature and history – all those various outputs of man which are vaguely lumped together as civilisation'. This, and other similar, authored series, became known as 'sledgehammers'. They would open the path for Attenborough himself to front shows with a similar approach, but focused on the natural world.

*

During his years at the BBC, Attenborough made countless big decisions. Inevitably, some of them do not look wise with the benefit of hindsight.

In 1965, as controller of BBC2, he 'politely rebuffed' an application from Terry Wogan, who wanted to become a presenter on the channel. Wogan, then working with Irish broadcaster RTE, said in his application that he 'should like to extend the sphere of my television activities', adding that he wished to see whether 'the success which I have enjoyed in Ireland can be translated to British television'.

However, it was a 'no' from Attenborough. 'I am afraid that, at the moment, we do not have any vacancy for

anyone with your particular talents and experience,' said Attenborough in his reply to the Irishman's application. He added that the network already had a chief announcer who was from Dublin. 'We would feel, other things being equal, that we should look for someone from a different part of the country, if we were to make an additional appointment,' he wrote.

Wogan went on to enjoy a 50-year career on radio and television, including presenting *Wake up to Wogan* on

BBC Radio 2 and the *Wogan* chat show on BBC1. Working for the BBC for the majority of his career, he was also the voice of Eurovision in the UK for many years and was pivotal to the Children in Need appeal from its beginnings in 1980. Upon Wogan's death in 2016, BBC Radio 2 controller Bob Shennan said he was 'one of the greatest and most popular radio hosts this country has ever heard'.

Told of the fateful correspondence when it was unearthed from the BBC archives decades later, Attenborough said: 'Good Lord! He wrote asking me for work? I don't remember this at all.' He added that, even though he met the Irish presenter many times in subsequent years, Sir Terry never mentioned the rejection letter.

★

Attenborough said that one of his biggest regrets during his management years was dropping Alan Bennett's sketches while controller at the BBC. Bennett, an English actor, author, playwright and screenwriter, had penned countless popular sketch shows and plays.

'One of the scars on my conscience is that the Alan Bennett programmes, which were wonderful, are not recorded and were lost,' he said.

He explained that someone at the corporation approached him and said: 'Look, we have to build another set of vaults and it's going to cost x million pounds.' They explained that would be the price tag if they were to keep all the bulky tapes of shows, adding: 'So can't you please find a way to keep the jewels and get rid of the dross?'

So a culling of some of the archives was ordered. 'That doesn't mean to say we shouldn't have kept some of the Alan Bennetts; we should,' he said.

*

DID YOU KNOW?

David's sister-in-law, Sheila Sim, was an English film and theatre actress. She acted alongside her husband, Richard Attenborough, in the 1948 film *The Guinea Pig*.

★

In 1960, Attenborough produced and presented a six-part series called *The People of Paradise*. On the shows, he taught viewers about the people and geography of Oceania, particularly Fiji and Tonga.

A part of the show was by royal appointment: Attenborough was personally invited to the region by the reigning monarch of Tonga, Queen Salote, to attend the Tongan Royal Kava Ceremony.

The series featured him marvelling at a diving custom performed by male islanders in the New Hebrides (now Vanuatu); members of the John Frum cargo cult in Tanna; the firewalkers of Beqa island, Fiji; and a tribal leader on the volcanic island of Koro, also in Fiji.

Also included were coconut crabs and fruit bats in Tonga and behind-the-scenes footage of the aforementioned Royal Kava Ceremony.

★

In December 1972, Attenborough wrote a memo calling for 'voices, attitudes and opinions that, for one reason or another, have been unheard or seriously neglected by mainstream programmes' to be included on the BBC. He had been influenced by an appeal for such content from Rowan Ayers, the creator of *Late Night Line-Up, The Old Grey Whistle Test* and *Up Sunday*. Ayers convinced Attenborough, who convinced the corporation. The results would be spectacular and eccentric.

The Community Programme Unit was founded and its main production, *Open Door*, featured everything from a trans lady sitting in her bath talking to a cat, to ufologists, to a man in an ape suit.

The title sequence of the show promised to offer people 'Your own say . . . in your own way'. The output was vast and frequently hard-hitting. One show, 'presented by a group of black schoolteachers', gave British viewers 'an early education in the idea of institutional racism', said the *Telegraph*, but a 1976 broadcast by the British Stop Immigration Group accused British Asians of 'spreading venereal disease and TB', noted the paper.

★

Another show featured The Aetherius Society, in which members of the society showed how to capture and relay spiritual energy, while the Albion Free State, a group of anarchists from west London, declared: 'Reality is a substitute for utopia. Politics is a substitute for instinct. Consumption is a substitute for feeling. Television is a substitute for telepathy.'

Looking back on the series in 2023, cultural historian Matthew Harle told *The Guardian*: 'What is striking now is how many of the subjects they tackled – immigration, housing, workers' rights – resonate strongly today.'

★

The final curtain of Attenborough's career has been discussed almost as many times as he has discussed the wildlife of the world. However, somehow the final day never seemed to come. During a meeting at the BBC studios on Whiteladies Road in Bristol in the late 1980s, producers discussed the imminent retirement of Attenborough, who was nearing the age of 65.

'We need to think about who is going to take over from David when this series is finished,' a junior producer, Mike Gunton, remembered his manager saying. Three decades later, with Attenborough still going strong, Gunton told *The Guardian*: 'We still haven't got an answer and I don't want one.'

David in colour

David Attenborough remembers vividly when he first saw a colour television set. It was during experimental sessions at BBC2, long before the general public got their hands on this breakthrough gadget.

At the end of the evening he visited a 'little studio' for the programme *Late Night Line-Up*, which went out live. They used three cameras, 'from different makes', so they could see the broadcast in both colour, and black and white. 'I had one of the first colour television sets in the country, which was about the size of a very large suitcase – an immense thing,' he said.

On it, he would watch colour television from *Late Night Line-Up* and phone the chief engineer for feedback. The engineer told Attenborough: 'Look, I don't want you programme people doing mad things, what I want is to get flesh tones right. That's the key thing.'

Attenborough said the chief engineer 'was quite right, of course' because 'if a man turned up with a scarlet face, it was no good'.

'He and I, only, in the entire Europe, were watching colour television broadcasts,' said Attenborough. Eventually, the chief engineer phoned with a specific request: 'David, I think it was very good last night,' he said. 'I think we could risk using a bowl of fruit.'

*

Journalists were invited to a special viewing of colour television at Television Centre. They were impressed with the new technology and the quality of the picture. Attenborough announced that the channel would initially broadcast in colour about five hours a week. Within months, 80 per cent of programmes were in colour.

Once people started to have colour televisions in their homes, they became a demanding demographic, he remembered. 'Anybody who invested in a colour television set had the thing on all the time and was ringing up and saying, "Why isn't this programme in colour?" because we couldn't do them all.'

*

Snooker did not take off on British television until the late 1960s and the man responsible for this breakthrough was Sir David Attenborough. The game had been covered occasionally in the early days of BBC radio, and was later featured on black-and-white television in the 1950s and 1960s.

Then, as controller of BBC2 in the late 1960s, Attenborough wanted to find a format to show off the ground-breaking invention of colour television. He decided snooker was the perfect thing. The colourful balls on a snooker table set off by the green baize of the table itself made the game a good choice for the early days of colour television. The fact that it was a low-budget and low-risk option didn't hurt its appeal to the TV bosses, either.

The idea was streamlined by broadcaster Ted Lowe, who came up with an idea for a new show. *Pot Black*

consisted of eight players, competing in a one-frame knockout tournament. The first episode was broadcast on 23 July 1969, three days after Neil Armstrong first walked on the moon.

*

Snooker was not the only sport in which Attenborough oversaw a broadcasting breakthrough. It was he who was in charge of the first colour broadcast of the Wimbledon tennis championships.

'Nobody else had got colour television and so everybody was watching it,' he explained 50 years later, remembering how 'very exciting' it was.

He added that 'there was a great hoo-hah about the bottles by the umpire's chair. They didn't look much in black and white, but in colour you could see it was lime cordial or whatever it was.'

He had heard on the grapevine that advertisers were 'paying people to go and twist the bottles so the labels were visible, and then we were doing the same thing – sending our people down to turn them back again,' he said. 'It was full of stuff like that.'

★

In the 1967 Wimbledon Men's Singles semifinal, West Germany's Wilhelm Bungert beat Britain's Roger Taylor to reach the final. There was an irony in this, as West Germany was one of the countries that Attenborough had competed against to become the first European broadcaster to launch a regular colour service.

'I heard the West Germans were doing it and I discovered that they were planning to launch it very close to when we were,' he said. 'But what I couldn't do [in that amount of time] was to start a complete kind of service. The best that I could do would be to have what I called a piebald service, so there was some colour every night, but the whole service wasn't in colour.'

This realization gave him the edge, and thanks to Attenborough the UK got colour television just weeks before West Germany. 'I was as proud as a peacock,' he said. 'It was absolutely terrific. It was a big moment in my life.'

*

In 2019, David noted how his role in the programmes had evolved over the years. He explained how, 40 years previously, he had travelled around the world three times as he made the *Life on Earth* TV series and that he wrote the script, and every page of the accompanying book.

'But now I just write and speak the words,' he confessed. When people asked him what it was like as animals were charging in, he replied: 'I wasn't there. Thirty cameramen worked on this thing.' Reflecting on this, he said he was 'given credit for things I don't do' and he was 'grateful', but 'also embarrassed'.

3

The Broadcasting Titan

Household name

Who can understand better the influence and importance of wildlife broadcasting than the man who has been synonymous with that sphere for as long as any of us can remember? Sir David measures that influence in the only way he knows how: in animals.

He remembered that when he started in television, 'it's difficult to believe it but creatures like pangolins or sloths or armadillos were really quite unknown to the general public. Now of course, everybody knows what they are, and why? Not because of me particularly, but because of television.'

Attenborough added: 'Television has told the world about the wild population, the wild part of the world, and that's essential that we know about it and we know how it works, and we understand why it is that we are damaging it so badly.'

It was as clear a summary as one can imagine of the power and importance of the medium he has been immersed in for decades.

*

In 1975, Attenborough wrote and presented a seven-part series called *The Tribal Eye*. It ranged from the life and customs of the Dogon people in Mali, to the art and cultures of the First Nations peoples of the Pacific Northwest of North America, to the tribal art of carpet-making in Persia (modern Iran).

Having explored all this and more, Attenborough concluded by examining the commercialization of tribal art. He had spent more than two years travelling 40,000km (25,000 miles) and visiting 16 countries to film the series.

Explaining what inspired him to make the series at the time, he told the *New York Times* that he 'realized that, though you can analyse a society and photograph it, its art is a way of understanding people that you can get in no other way, particularly if you know how and why the art is made.'

He added: 'It occurred to me that these objects were made with passion, certainly with deep emotion, and there was very deep significance to them. I wanted to show this art.'

★

Another venture from this time was a children's TV series called *Fabulous Animals*. For a generation of TV-watching schoolchildren, it was a lovely and popular show that became appointment viewing.

Looking back on the series, *ForteanTimes* magazine said it had a 'Pythonesque, illuminated manuscript title sequence and blaring trumpet theme', and featured 'an earnest and still youthful-looking David Attenborough zipping through a panoply of monster stories covering everything from mammoths locked in ice to Bigfoot'.

★

DID YOU KNOW?

The first series of *Planet Earth* took five years to produce and was at the time the most expensive series ever commissioned by the BBC.

Life on Earth

The landmark series *Life on Earth* was first broadcast on 16 January 1979. It was a bold, ambitious attempt to transfer the authored approach that Kenneth Clark took with *Civilisation* to the natural world. It took three years to film and became absolutely synonymous with Attenborough.

His historic opening narration told viewers that: 'There are some four million different kinds of animals and plants in the world. Four million different solutions to the problems of staying alive. This is the story of how a few of them came to be as they are.'

★

To make the series, Attenborough visited more than 30 countries and travelled nearly 2.4 million kilometres (1.5 million miles) in the process. All that effort was worthwhile: it was watched by more than 500 million people worldwide.

★

The theme tune for the series was composed by the British composer Edward Williams. It used flute, harp, clarinet, strings, percussion and early synthesizers. The host thoroughly approved. 'I think it added to the programme very well,' Attenborough said later. 'It's very different from a huge orchestra, it has an almost chamber music sound.'

★

DID YOU KNOW?

The *Life on Earth* book, put together to accompany the TV series, was published on what would have been Charles Darwin's 170th birthday. It was a fitting date because Attenborough has always been fascinated by Darwin. 'Why should there be such a dazzling variety?' he later asked, referring to the range of life forms on Earth. 'And how can we make sense of such a huge range of living organisms? 200 years ago, a man was born who was to explain this astonishing diversity of life. In doing so, he revolutionized the way in which we see the world and our place in it. His name was Charles Darwin.'

*

Attenborough, who has covered the life of butterflies in several series including *Life on Earth* and the BBC Radio 4 series *David Attenborough's Life Stories*, is the president of Butterfly Conservation.

*

During the filming of an episode of *Life on Earth*, Attenborough was demonstrating the colour of the snow when he slipped, and slid down a mountainside. He was unhurt by the accident and agreed magnanimously to allow footage of the fall to be shown in a montage of outtakes in his memoir *Life on Air*.

*

Five years after *Life on Earth* came *The Living Planet*. It examined the ways in which living organisms, including human beings, adapt to their surroundings.

'Our planet, the Earth, is, as far as we know, unique in the universe,' began his opening narration. 'Two-thirds of the surface of this unique planet are covered by water, and it was here indeed that life began,' he explained. 'From the oceans, it has spread even to the summits of the highest mountains as animals and plants have responded to the changing face of the Earth.'

*

It was a challenging series to make. For instance, when they went to Sudan they discovered there were no conventional roads there. When they shot in the Himalayas they had to walk all the way. When they filmed in South America, a scarcity of boats meant one cameraman had to push his equipment in a rubber dinghy while swimming behind it.

As ever, though, Attenborough was self-effacing about his own role in the series, insisting that it was not hard for him. 'The difficulties are not actually experienced by me, because the bits that I do are the easiest bits,' he said. 'It's not too difficult to walk on to a rock and look at a camera and say something. The difficulties are those that are encountered by the cameramen, directors and recordists, who actually have to get an animal doing something which perhaps nobody's ever even seen before. Those are extremely difficult things to do.'

*

In the 1984 documentary *The Making of The Living Planet*, the humorous broadcaster Miles Kington introduced Attenborough in much the same way as Attenborough would introduce a creature. It turned the tables on Sir David with respect and admiration, as well as humour.

'One thing that distinguishes men from other living creatures is that only men make films about other living creatures, and perhaps one of the most famous and interesting of these film makers is the species known as David Attenborough,' Kington quipped.

'Somewhat shy and not always easy to film in his natural habitat, we're lucky here to see the David Attenborough at work on his latest and greatest project, *The Living Planet*.'

Added Kington: 'He enjoys this rather strange, symbiotic relationship with the BBC, an odd and apparently friendly organism, whose workings we do not yet fully understand . . .'

★

DID YOU KNOW?

David Attenborough is thought to be one of the most travelled human beings in history. For the 1998 series *Life of Birds* alone, he travelled 412,000km (256,000 miles) by air.

Loss and Reflection

In 1997, tragedy struck when Attenborough's wife, Jane, collapsed with a brain haemorrhage on the eve of their 47th wedding anniversary. He was on the other side of the world, filming in New Zealand, when it happened, but as soon as he heard the news, he dashed home to be at her bedside.

To his horror, he found her in a coma, when a doctor suggested he hold her hand. 'She did, and gave my hand a squeeze,' he wrote in his memoir, *Life on Air*. It proved to be their final interaction: Jane died soon after. 'The focus of my life, the anchor had gone . . . Now I was lost.'

He had lost and he was lost – it took him a great deal of strength, effort and time to come to terms with it. Reflecting upon grief and the loneliness that comes with it, he said some years later: 'You accommodate things . . . you deal with things. I'm quite used to solitude in the wilds but, no, an empty house is not what I enjoy. But my daughter's there. In moments of grief – deep grief – the only consolation you can find is in the natural world.'

★

As he came to terms with the loss of his beloved wife, Attenborough found that immersing himself in work was a great help and comfort to him. When a person loses their spouse or partner during retirement, the bereavement may leave a noticeable gap. Attenborough, who rarely speaks about his wife and her loss, explained that his way was different.

'I coped by working,' he said. 'It was the most fantastic luck that I was able to work. If my life had gone a different way – say I had gone into the oil business, which I once considered doing – I would have been out at 60.'

What a loss it would have been to the world had Attenborough 'gone into the oil business' rather than becoming all he has become.

*

Being a widow or widower often means you become a lot more lonely, and he spoke about the curse of loneliness in much the same way as he speaks about nature – in simple but touching terms.

'I would rather have people around,' he said. 'The thing is, when you go around the house, you know that, no matter how many doors you open there is not going to be anybody there, and that's a pity. Then you go down to have a meal that you have to cook for yourself, which is not too odd, but, you know, it is nice to be able to talk to someone.'

*

The loss of Jane has given David lots of time and cause for reflection on grief and bereavement. He has burrowed deep into his feelings, to gain a greater understanding of those twin challenges of life.

For instance, he reflected: 'In moments of great grief, that's where you look and immerse yourself. You realize you are not immortal, you are not a god, you are part of the natural world and you come to accept that.'

*

So, what, according to Attenborough, is the ultimate meaning of life? 'It seems to me that an understanding of the natural world is crucial for all of us – after all, we depend upon it for our food, for the air we breathe and, some would say, for our very sanity.'

*

In terms of his relationship with religion and faith, he says he considers himself an agnostic, rather than an atheist. 'I don't think an understanding and an acceptance of the four-billion-year-long history of life is any way inconsistent with a belief in a supreme being,' he said. 'And I am not so confident as to say that I am an atheist.'

*

When his brother, Richard, died in 2014, Attenborough paid fulsome tribute to him. 'Dick was a marvellous comic actor,' he said. 'He was very, very funny, and could be – and was – in domestic circumstances. We just spent all our time roaring with laughter – and that didn't get much of an outlet in his feature films.'

Some of his fondest memories of his brother came at Christmas time. 'You know, we just sat around, roaring with laughter,' he said.

At a memorial service in 2015, David read from Richard's maiden speech in the House of Lords: 'The arts are not a prerequisite of the privileged few; nor are they the playground of the intelligentsia. The arts are for everyone – and failure to include everyone diminishes us all.'

He is so proud of his late brother, though he had been less than happy when Richard was cast as serial killer John Christie in the 1971 film *10 Rillington Place*. 'I couldn't bear to watch my dear brother imitating a sexual murderer,' he said. 'I just didn't want to see it; I'm too fond of my brother.'

The funny side

Although he remains the cuddly, wholesome grandfather to a nation, he has occasionally shown a cheeky side. A good example is when he appeared on *The Graham Norton Show* in 2015, along with the actress Jessica Chastain.

Attenborough said on the show that he had explained in a documentary what male birds of paradise do 'to ingratiate themselves to the female birds', adding that they 'hang upside down and whistle and they have long quills coming out of their tail which they flick across the face of the female'.

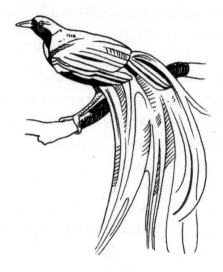

Chastain said: 'That wouldn't impress me at all.'

To great laughter, Attenborough replied: 'It would. I can show you later!'

★

He has proven to be quite the raconteur when it comes to the chat-show circuit and also had the audience giggling during an appearance in 2013 on *The Jonathan Ross Show*. When he told Ross about his dislike of rats, the host asked how he reacts when he sees one, and Sir David said: 'Throw a boot at it!'

He then presented Ross with a (caged) scorpion. 'Even if he stung you, it wouldn't kill you,' he assured him. 'If you interfered with him at the front, he would bring that forward and sting you,' he said, prompting Ross to reply: 'Can I pick this up?'

With perfect understatement, Attenborough said: 'Well, you can if you like. Personally, I would be careful. A sting is a sting.'

*

As a broadcasting titan, he has become a widely referred-to figure on the small screen – including on reality television.

On an episode of *Britain's Got Talent,* judge Simon Cowell launched into an unexpected impersonation of Attenborough. Giving his verdict on schoolboy Aneeshwar Kunchala's powerful poem about the environment, Cowell assumed an Attenborough-style delivery, to say: 'Aneeshwar, I would like you to take over from me doing *Blue Planet*.'

Just months later, the BBC's *Strictly Come Dancing* featured a dance routine influenced by the *Planet Earth* series and narrated by Sir David. In it, the show's movers and shakers took on the roles of earth, fire, air and water to pay tribute to the natural world.

*

Attenborough's voice is one of the most iconic and recognizable in broadcasting. It has been widely imitated but even more widely praised. 'The voice is like a piano played gently,' wrote Giles Smith, in the *Daily Telegraph*, after he interviewed Sir David.

*

DID YOU KNOW?

The producers of his television shows affectionately refer to him as 'SDA'.

★

A Finnish heavy metal band once wrote to Attenborough, asking him to speak on their album. Although he turned down the request, he left the rockers impressed by his good manners and politeness.

'We wrote him a letter and he wrote one back, declining, but it was very impressive that a man of his stature would write personally to us and explain that he just didn't have the time right now,' said singer Floor Jansen of Nightwish.

★

Attenborough did get involved in the music scene on other occasions. In 2015, he narrated the singer–songwriter Adele's hit 'Hello'. During a BBC radio show, the host, Greg James, had suggested that Attenborough narrate the single's promotional video.

At first, Attenborough had appeared apprehensive and asked: 'Really? Will Adele be cross with me?' James replied: 'I think Adele would probably love this more than anything in the whole world.'

David kicked off the narration with: 'The year is 2015. The world appears to have a green tint to it, but there are also some dead insects in the foreground, but don't worry about that for now.'

He then went on to describe Adele as a 'delicate and finely tuned animal' who is 'about to be everywhere again'. In a particularly humorous moment, he referred to the fact that she used an old-fashioned mobile phone on the video, a topic that had already been discussed widely on social media. 'The weather is poor and she hasn't upgraded her handset since 1999,' he said. 'Hashtag flip phone.'

*

Attenborough also turned his commentating gravitas to the sporting arena. Egged on again by BBC DJ Greg James, and purely for a giggle, he narrated the Women's Curling final at the 2014 Sochi Winter Olympics:

'Watch as the alpha female displays her dominance over the herd by tapping the head of the frisking broom to check for rogue insects. And off she goes, gently but flamboyantly launching the over-sized walnut down the frozen river.'

He continued: 'The alpha female's job is now complete. It's down to the herd to frantically follow the walnut down the river, gently frisking the foreground. The frisking is frantic and often futile, making no difference to the success of the net thrust. But it's playful, and all part of what makes this game the sliding curlers play so magical.'

It was great fun and had viewers in stitches.

★

DID YOU KNOW?

A rave in Birmingham in 2022 featured revellers wearing masks of Sir David as they danced all night. Called the David Attenborough Jungle Rave, and boasting a jungle setting with inflatable monkeys, lions and giraffes, it was quite a spectacle.

Extraordinary adventures

In 2015, Attenborough spoke of his record-breaking 1,600-m (1,000-ft) dive that year in a submersible on the Great Barrier Reef, during the making of a programme named after the reef. With plentiful charm, he made the challenging experience seem almost cosy.

'It's jolly nice someone of my age can be taken down in comfort, 1,000 feet down . . . nobody else had gone down that far before,' he told the BBC director-general, Tony Hall, during an interview on stage.

'We had no idea what to expect or what we might see,' he said, but the experience turned out to be like 'being in a cinema or something'.

Attenborough added: 'You're in absolute comfort, you're not strapped in . . . the temperature's the same, you don't have to worry about breathing, you're just there munching chocolates saying "this is wonderful".'

A less comfortable aspect of the experience was the lack of . . . toilet facilities. However, submersible pilot

Mark 'Buck' Taylor said that this had been planned for and that if anyone needed to answer the call of nature during the dive, a receptacle would be provided and towels could be held up for dignity as 'we've got cameras pointing from every direction'.

*

This was not the first time that Attenborough had filmed at the Reef. Indeed, his previous experience there had been magical and memorable for him.

'People say to me, "What was the most magical thing you ever saw in your life?"' he said. 'And I always say without a word of exaggeration, "the first time I was lucky enough to scuba dive on the Great Barrier Reef".'

He had wanted to visit the Reef since he was a boy and he saw a 'whopping great book' called the *The Great Barrier Reef of Australia* by William Saville-Kent, published in 1893, with 'wonderful hand-coloured illustrations inside'.

In 1957, when he was preparing to pass Australia on the way to New Guinea, he realized 'there's a chance here, boy' to visit the Reef. He took a three-day course learning how to use an aqualung in a Royal Navy tank, and the next thing he knew he was on the Barrier Reef.

When in 2015 he was reshown the footage of that 1957 trip, he poked fun at himself and his changing appearance: 'My impression of course is that I still look like that! It just happens that today is a bit of a bad day.'

*

As we now know, Attenborough is very frightened of rats. However, they are not the only creatures that have unsettled him as he has roamed the planet for our viewing pleasure.

'I think the most alarming animals I have encountered are really poisonous snakes,' he said. 'I have seen a king cobra. They go toward people, they rear up six feet tall and they're very aggressive and they are very fast. And one bite means certain death. So if I encountered a king cobra in the wild I would be very alarmed.'

It seems a reasonable reaction. Who wouldn't be?

*

Asked which animal he had found most difficult to document during his long career, Attenborough said: 'I nominate going to look for mountain gorillas for the first time. That was an unforgettable time and more successful than we could possibly have hoped . . . but it was a long time ago.'

In the *Life on Earth* episode, filmed in 1978 in Rwanda and broadcast the next year, he was surprised to find himself up close and personal with an adult gorilla who was staring him in the face. The following day, when Attenborough returned, the same adult female and her two young chose to play with him, grooming him and stealing his shoes.

During the 2007 documentary *Gorillas Revisited*, he watched the old footage of himself playing with the baby gorillas. 'You can't talk about the opposable thumb and the importance in primate evolution of the grip if somebody's taking off your shoes. Particularly if that somebody is two baby gorillas.'

★

Sometimes Attenborough is present when a rare animal is filmed in a distant location, but at other times his contribution is to record narration over footage filmed by others. He has admitted that he can be left confused over which animals he encountered in person and which he watched from a studio.

'You can say to Martyn Colbeck, a great wildlife cameraman, "Go to Sulawesi. There's a kind of aberrant pig which I saw in a book but which nobody seems to have got good pictures of." And Martyn goes and gets it. And then it comes back, and before long, by the time I've viewed it, edited it, written the words for it, I've convinced myself I've seen it. I can't remember whether I was there or I wasn't.'

★

DID YOU KNOW?

David Attenborough has said, if he could have any superpower, it would be to 'fly under my own volition'.

*

Speaking of hypothetical scenarios, he once said that if he could opt to bring back to life any extinct creature, he would choose the biggest-known pterosaur, called the quetzalcoatlus, which lived at the same time as dinosaurs.

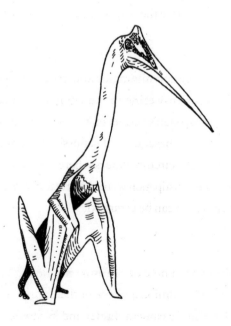

Named an 'absurd creature' by *Wired* magazine, it stood as tall as a giraffe and had the body of a bat and the head and neck of a stork.

With a 12-m (40-ft) wingspan, they were 'wonderful, flying monsters', beamed Attenborough. 'Some [pterosaurs] were as big as crows, but others, like the quetzalcoatlus, were the size of small airplanes.'

★

Filming on location in jungles and other hazardous terrains makes answering the call of nature tricky at times. Attenborough's verdict on this is as understated and Attenborougheseque as it is possible to imagine. 'There are some circumstances where the loos are so appalling that constipation would be preferable,' he said. 'But constipation can be arranged.'

★

There have been no end of funny moments during Attenborough's filming and one of them came when a lyrebird imitated a camera shutter and its motor drive, in the 1998 series *The Life of Birds*. The extraordinary scene sees the bird imitating the songs of other birds it hears in the jungle. It then duplicates perfectly the other sounds it has heard, including the sound of a camera shutter, a car alarm and a chainsaw felling trees. The moment was the winner of a national viewer poll, held in 2008, to choose the best Attenborough clips of all time.

But another contender for that title came when the world's largest species of grouse knocked Attenborough off his feet, as he entered its territory in the Caledonian pine forest of the Scottish Highlands.

He was trying to explain how, its 'being the breeding season', the bird would 'display at almost anything – including me', before finding himself abruptly pushed to the ground. With a schoolteacher air, he told the bird: 'Now, now.'

★

During an interview event in 2013, Attenborough was asked what creature had scared him most during his television career. 'A man, who is drunk, who doesn't speak your language, who doesn't like the look of your face,' he said. 'That's the scariest thing I've ever seen.'

★

David holds an estimated 32 honorary degrees from universities throughout the UK, more than anyone else.

He was named a doctor of science by Durham University and a doctor of philosophy by the University of Oxford. In 2013, after he was given an honorary degree by Queen's University in Belfast, he was asked by a reporter how many degrees he had.

Modestly avoiding the question, he smiled and said it would be 'rude to count'.

*

All the degrees and honours he has been awarded mean he has many dozens of letters after his name. At the last count, his name and titles read: David Attenborough, OM GCMG CH CVO CBE FRS FSA FRSA FLS FZS FRSGS FRSB.

Again, he prefers to make light of it, saying that 'honorary degrees are just about having someone well known at a ceremony'.

'That's something that's out of fashion now, putting letters after your name,' he told an interviewer, adding that 'half of those are insignificant'. He said his OM

(Order of Merit) 'has got to be significant' but said, 'I don't think young people rate that sort of thing at all.'

Loved and adored

During his 70 years of broadcasting, Attenborough has seen all forms of life and witnessed some breathtaking species. With every film, he has narrated the scenes perfectly. But one encounter, on an Asian island, left him speechless.

'We were in Borneo,' he recalled. 'I was there because I wanted to climb Mount Kinabalu. Coming down, there were these two girls and they recognized me.

'One said, "I want to show you something." And there was a tattoo of my face on her upper outer thigh.'

★

British documentary-maker Louis Theroux has interviewed a galaxy of stars, from wholesome household names to disgraced public figures. He once quizzed Attenborough for *Radio Times*, noting how cooperative his subject was.

'He was, as one would expect, on time, obliging, friendly, and unperturbed by the photographer's directions that I should stand ever closer to him and peer into his left ear,' wrote Theroux, 'and then (more embarrassingly) that we should gaze at each other nose-to-nose like boxers, while being asked for "more warmth".'

Theroux wrote: 'I came away feeling I'd had a close encounter with one of the big beasts of the broadcasting jungle, a species that is increasingly endangered and all the more precious for that.'

Speaking to Theroux, David opened up about his regret over missing his children's formative years. 'If I do have regrets, it is that when my children were the same age as your children, I was away for three months at a time,' he said. 'If you have a child of six or eight and you miss three months of his or her life, it's irreplaceable; you miss something.'

★

A cameraman who had worked with Attenborough gave his verdict on how to manage the veteran broadcaster.

'Give him a glass of wine and some chocolate and he's happy,' the cameraman told Louis Theroux.

Told of the quote, Attenborough chuckled and said: 'Actually, I've given up chocolate.'

Explaining why, he said he was 'eating too much of it!' He added: 'I could easily eat half a pound of Cadbury's Fruit & Nut, at a sitting, without noticing. And I suddenly thought, "This is ridiculous. You've got to stop it."'

*

Asked what his philosophy for work was, Attenborough said: 'Take it! Just do it.' It's not quite the 'Just Do It' slogan of the Nike sportswear brand, but close enough.

*

Despite his warm and (almost) cuddly nature, Attenborough can be stern when the mood takes him or the situation requires it. When an interviewer from *The Times* asked Attenborough who he voted for, he said Attenborough 'chastised' him, telling him that it was a 'private vote'.

His crew can attest that Attenborough is as human as the rest of us and therefore has his more severe side. 'I have felt the wrath of mighty David – when you literally get that look and shrivel,' said his cameraman, Gavin Thurston. 'A look is enough. Like a silverback when they do that tight-lipped thing. You just know.'

★

In 2019, a YouGov poll found Attenborough was the most popular person in Britain.

★

In 2023, Attenborough and his team found themselves the subject of a novel accusation: that they produced 'slug porn'.

The i Paper's arts and media correspondent, Adam Sherwin, said that the *Wild Isles* series 'features extra lashings of sex to compensate for a shortage of dramatic hunting footage', adding that 'penises have loomed large in the hit BBC One natural history series'.

DID YOU KNOW?

If Attenborough could be any animal, he'd be a sloth. However, the animal he has said he feels the most kinship with is an ape, because 'our kinship is a reality'. He added: 'I don't feel it with a mosquito or, indeed, a whale.'

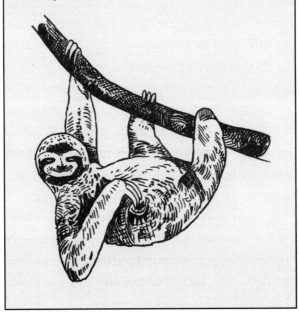

One scene featured the sex lives of Dartmoor's ash-back slugs, with Sir David explaining how the hermaphrodite molluscs have both male and female sexual organs, and mate by hanging from a branch and twisting together.

He said they form a 'magical pendulum of love', as two penises protruded, each as long as its owner's 30cm (12in) body, wrapping around each other as sperm is passed between them.

Chris Howard, the series producer, said: 'We put a lot of thought in how to pitch it.' He added: 'It's important to engage a young audience. We need to serve an audience from age five to 85 – and older than that, because David is 96 – so it is difficult to toe the line and keep everyone happy.'

★

DID YOU KNOW?

So many Chinese viewers downloaded *Blue Planet II* that it temporarily slowed down the country's internet.

In 2023, Attenborough was getting as many as 50 letters from children each day, he said. The letters were frequently opinionated, rather than cute.

'Children now don't write to me about *The Wind in the Willows*,' he explained. 'They write about the real things. How disgusted they were when they walked along the beach with their mummy and picked up a sack of plastic.'

★

You might expect that watching Attenborough's programmes makes viewers more interested in nature, and a study has confirmed that to be true.

Researchers from University College Dublin who were investigating whether nature documentaries can promote plant awareness focused on *The Green Planet*, a 2022 BBC documentary narrated by Sir David.

When certain species appeared on *The Green Planet* there was a 'substantial effect' on online searches for those species, they noted. Commenting on the correlation, the study's lead author said: 'I think that increasing public awareness of plants is essential and fascinating.'

*

Is there a more praised broadcaster in Britain than Sir David? Time after time, the media lauds him to the hilt. In 2010, *The Guardian* heaped praise on Attenborough in a leader comment, saying he had 'led the world on an intellectual voyage of discovery'.

'He taught the world to value diversity and sensitized us to the delicacy of different environments,' said the paper. 'He tilled the ground for the case for climate change. And in making the natural world a place without borders, he has repeatedly challenged the boundaries of television itself.'

Age is just a number

Like anyone who reaches such an advanced age, Attenborough has outlived many people he cherished. But this has made him more determined to carry on with his work.

'A lot of my friends and relations are dead but the fact that I can still work and put two words together, well, I ought to take advantage of it,' he said. 'It's a gift.'

*

However, he does not continue to work out of fear that his life would be empty without work. 'I would be perfectly happy to go on watching spiders in my garden,' he said in 2017. 'I'm just delighted that people should ask me to do these things.'

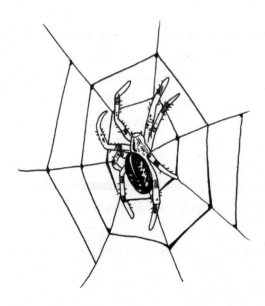

*

Attenborough has been conscious about his body and its decline as he gets older. Asked what single thing would improve the quality of his life, he replied: 'Good, workable knees.'

*

His knees might not be as 'workable' as he wishes, but his body has allowed him to stay more active than most people his age. He does not take this for granted. 'I'm fantastically lucky. I can hardly believe it's true,' he said. 'Here I am in my mid 90s and I'm still as active as I was in my 60s, or my 30s even. It is amazing that one can carry on.'

*

Part of Attenborough's charm is his informal appearance and childlike air. When he was interviewed by the *Daily Telegraph* in 2016, Joe Shute, the journalist, documented these sides of the national treasure.

'His hair has been whipped into the crest of a silver wave by the winds howling about London's West End outside,' wrote Shute, adding that 'his crumpled linen shirt appears to have resisted the valiant attempts of an iron'.

'When he notices a KitKat (his favourite treat) left for him on the table in the room we have been allotted at the BBC, he lights up in boyish enthusiasm,' wrote Shute. The love of chocolate may never fully leave him.

★

DID YOU KNOW?

David Attenborough doesn't own a car, as he never passed his driving test. He's also not a big fan of sending emails, and prefers receiving letters by fax or post.

When he was making *Wild Isles*, Attenborough enjoyed the two trips to the island of Skomer, off the west coast of Wales, where he filmed with puffins and Manx shearwater chicks.

Alastair Fothergill, the series producer, who has worked with Attenborough for 35 years, remembered how agile the nonagenarian was.

'There are around 67 steep steps from where you get off the boat to when you reach the first path at the top of the island,' said Fothergill. 'For all of us, especially with all our very heavy camera kit, those steps were something of a challenge. But David managed them amazingly despite his 96 years.'

★

More gravely, Fothergill also revealed that there was a moment when the 96-year-old could have died during the filming of the series.

The incident came when they were filming in the middle of the night on Skomer, waiting for a Manx shearwater chick to take flight for the first time for a migration to South America.

A local warden suggested a way to get good footage of Attenborough. 'If you sit David close to the burrows, they will almost certainly climb up his arm, onto his head and take off from his head,' said the warden.

'We thought, "Wow, that could be TV gold,"' said Fothergill. But when they learned that avian flu was reportedly present on a neighbouring island, the producer consulted with a friend, a government adviser on infectious diseases, on how risky it would be for the elderly broadcaster.

He told Fothergill: 'If David gets it he will die, but it's actually very, very hard to get bird flu. As long as David is just by the bird, on the rock, it'll be fine.' The producer remarked that 'although everyone was happy', this revelation made it 'a bit unnerving'.

★

There was also a note of caution when Attenborough wanted to appear onscreen in a hang-glider in 2013. He explained: 'We're doing a film in 3D about how flight has evolved in animals . . . I wrote the script and I said I wanted to appear in a hang-glider and that I would be hang-gliding and then this thing with a 30ft wingspan would come from behind,' he said.

His plan was rejected because 'the insurance people wouldn't do it', he said.

★

Nick Gates, another producer on the *Wild Isles* series, said that Attenborough brought a unique perspective to the production because he is a 'phenomenal barometer of change'.

Added Gates: 'If you look at the natural history of Britain and Ireland, it has changed enormously over his lifetime and so it's very powerful when he talks about that.'

★

Joe Loncraine, who worked with Attenborough on the film *Light on Earth* in 2016, said that as a young man, his 'ultimate goal' was 'to work with Sir David Attenborough'. However, with Attenborough nearly 80 by the time Loncraine broke into the industry, he thought it was 'extremely unlikely' that this would happen.

So it was a 'veritable dream come true' when he got the chance. 'I think we were all positively shocked by how much David was still willing to get his hands dirty,' Loncraine said. 'David's energy and enthusiasm made me believe more than ever that age really is just a number and no longer reflects one's abilities or attitudes to life.'

He remembered Attenborough 'lying in a damp field in France, digging up worms from the ground at 10 o'clock at night' and considered him a 'genius storyteller' with an 'ability to transfer his enthusiasm for the natural world' that was 'second to none'.

*

When Attenborough discusses his remarkable television career, he does so without a hint of arrogance or entitlement. It is as if, even after his decades at the top of the tree, he still does not quite believe he is there, or even deserves to be there.

His viewers and fans would disagree. For them, it is only too right that Attenborough has remained in the spotlight for so long. Yet perhaps it is the fact that Sir David thinks himself lucky that makes him so popular. Either way, it has been quite a career.

'I have had the fortune to meet some of the planet's most enchanting creatures,' he said on *David Attenborough's Natural Curiosities*. 'But some stand out more than others because of their intriguing biology. Our knowledge of some of these creatures extends back centuries. Others we've discovered more recently.'

★

His televisual longevity has even been recognized by Guinness World Records. On the record-keeper's official website, Sir David is listed as having 'the longest career as a television naturalist'. Other Brits who have enjoyed long TV careers include the entertainer Sir Bruce Forsyth and astronomer Sir Patrick Moore.

4

Protector of the Planet

Fighting for nature

One of Sir David's most popular traits is the tenderness with which he speaks about the creatures we share our planet with. He casts them as what they are: creatures as deserving of understanding as any other. In doing so, he helps viewers understand what we have in common and why they, too, matter.

'Chimpanzees can show great kindness and compassion,' he said on the 2009 TV series *Nature's Great Events*. 'Sharing. Experimenting. Empathy. Planning. Intelligence. Teaching, and learning. Behaviour so characteristic of us higher primates.'

He continued: 'We are the most inventive and innovative of all primates. Just one branch of a large and extended family. A family which has refined the ability to develop and pass on individual learning to the next generation. A family which is built on strong bonds between mother and baby. A family with which we share so much.'

★

In a video filmed for *The Life of Mammals* in 2002 at Borneo's Camp Leakey, Attenborough introduced us to a family of orangutans that could paddle a boat, could wash socks and other clothes, and seemed to love do-it-yourself tasks such as bashing nails into wood. Another was seen sawing. He commented how 'striking' it was to see 'how similar they are to human beings'.

★

It seemed both fitting and inevitable that Attenborough, the best-known elderly advocate for the natural world, would eventually meet the world's most famous young climate crusader. Attenborough first met the environmental campaigner Greta Thunberg on a

Skype interview in 2019, as part of the teenager's guest editorship of the BBC's flagship *Today* news programme. Separated by many generations, the pair's summit nevertheless proved to be a meeting of minds.

He said Thunberg had 'achieved things that many of us who have been working on it for 20 odd years have failed to achieve. That is, you have aroused the world,' he told her. 'I'm very grateful to you. We all are, really.'

In response, Thunberg said: 'I think everyone is grateful for you, for taking on the climate crisis and on the environmental crisis.' She added that watching his 'documentaries about the natural world and what was happening' was 'what made me decide to do something about it'.

★

In 2022, Sir David was given a second knighthood for his services to both television and conservation. He was honoured for his work highlighting the natural world in TV shows and his campaigning to protect it.

Sir David received his new title at Windsor Castle on 9 June 2022, at a special ceremony carried out by Prince Charles (now Charles III).

As we have seen, he was first knighted by the Queen in 1985, but his second royal accolade appointed him Knight Grand Cross of the Order of St Michael and St George.

Just days before, he had been featured during the Platinum Party at the Palace, held outside Buckingham Palace as part of the Queen's 70th Jubilee weekend. He had given a speech while his face was projected onto the side of Buckingham Palace, after being referred to as a 'visionary environmentalist' by Prince William.

★

2022 proved to be a year of honour and note for Attenborough. Months before his second knighthood, he had been nominated for a Nobel Prize. He joined Pope Francis and the World Health Organization on the list of candidates for 2022.

Through his nomination, Attenborough had his name alongside such prominent dissidents as Sviatlana Tsikhanouskaya of Belarus and the jailed Russian opposition politician, Alexei Navalny.

Sir David was nominated by politicians in Norway for his 'efforts to inform about, and protect, Earth's natural diversity, a prerequisite for sustainable and peaceful societies'.

As the Norwegian nominators have a track record of suggesting the eventual recipient of the award, Attenborough was heavily fancied to take the gong. However, Ukrainian, Russian and Belarusian human rights campaigners turned out to be the joint winners of the 2022 Nobel Peace Prize.

★

Sir David has said that having plants and animals named after him is the 'biggest of compliments that you could ask from any scientific community'. At the last count, more than 50 organisms had been named after him, from *Attenborosaurus* (a plesiosaur) to *Spintharus davidattenboroughii* (a spider).

★

When he turned 90, Attenborough was cheered by some warm words of praise from Prince William, another moment of endorsement from the House of Windsor, which has kept an eye on him for so long.

'There is something very calming and warm about his programmes, something very reassuring about seeing him on BBC1,' said William. He said that Attenborough's content was 'part of the national psyche', and therefore it's 'very fitting' that he was having his 90th birthday 'a few weeks after the Queen'.

★

The Covid pandemic forced Attenborough to pause from his normal schedule of jetting around the globe. Instead, he stayed close to home in Richmond-upon-Thames.

Not that this meant that he stopped appreciating nature. In fact, it brought him closer to it. 'I can't actually remember taking three walks a day as I did almost every day this spring,' he said at the time. 'I was more aware of flowers opening, buds forming, birds arriving, than I have ever been. It was amazing.'

★

DID YOU KNOW?

David doesn't think of himself as an animal lover. To him, an animal lover means 'a cloying, anthropomorphizing sentiment'. He explains: 'I don't love earth worms or spiders. They're rivetingly interesting and they give me huge intellectual pleasure. And aesthetic pleasure, I suppose. But that's a different thing altogether.'

Speaking of noticing birds, he is a big fan of Oxford's Great Tit study, which was launched as far back as 1947. The longest continuous study of an individually marked animal population in the world, it is a project Attenborough thinks is marvellous.

In 2022, he said he was 'delighted' to hear of the 75th anniversary of this long-term study in Wytham Woods. 'Having visited several times, I know how fundamental this study, and others like it, have been for

our understanding of the impacts of climate change on the natural world,' he said.

'Long-term studies like this require long-term commitment, and I wish the study – and its practitioners – a long and productive future.'

*

Attenborough was also quick to acknowledge that, although lockdown brought challenges to him, 'many people are having a much worse time than I am'. Speaking to the BBC, he said: 'I am lucky. I have a garden, I have a house . . . my daughter and I are surviving very well.'

★

In 2019, David Attenborough voiced the Netflix series *Our Planet*, which highlighted some of the most pressing challenges facing nature today. At the premiere of the show, Attenborough gave a compelling speech: 'Nature once determined how we survive. Now we determine how nature survives.'

A word of warning

In a documentary on BBC iPlayer in 2023, Sir David warned that human beings have 'a few short years' left to 'make a choice' on how to recover the natural world.

Speaking in *Saving Our Wild Isles*, he said: 'In this film, we'll meet inspiring people, young and old, who are working to restore the natural world and we will discover that we all need to urgently repair our relationship with the natural world.'

He said that 'just enough remains of the natural world for it to recover' and that recovery 'starts and ends with us'.

*

In 2020, Sir David advised that the excesses of Western countries 'be curbed' to restore the natural world for the benefit of all, and that nature would flourish once again when 'those that have a great deal, perhaps, have a little less'.

He continued: 'We are going to have to live more economically than we do. And we can do that and, I believe, we will do it more happily, not less happily.' He was not arguing that 'capitalism is dead', he insisted, because he is 'not an economist'. However, he added: 'I believe the nations of the world, ordinary people worldwide, are beginning to realize that greed does not actually lead to joy.'

Attenborough offered these thoughts during the first year of the Covid pandemic. Lockdowns had forcibly slowed down many people's lives and led to much reflection on whether our consumption and pace of existence had been correctly configured. As ever, he had captured the moment well.

'We've had time to sit down', he said, and whether you were in the garden or the park, 'suddenly . . . there's a bird singing and I've not heard that for a bit . . . and that lifts the spirit to an extraordinary degree and you begin to realize what is really important'.

*

Attenborough admitted that he got out of his seat 'cheering all by myself' when Joe Biden beat Donald Trump in the 2020 White House election. However, he felt that, whoever was in the White House, they were going to have a tough time convincing some Americans that they would have to change their lifestyles to protect the planet.

He said: 'I filmed a year or so ago one of these series in a helicopter, flying up and down Miami, and I said to the pilot, "All these great huge hotels, if we go on like this they'll all be under water." "Rubbish," he said. He sees no reason why anyone should take any action.' Attenborough felt that there are some Americans 'who do not believe it, including the past president'.

★

In the UK in a 2017 interview, Attenborough commented on the Conservative politician Michael Gove's statement during the European Union referendum campaign that the public had 'had enough of experts'.

'That's a cry from somebody who doesn't understand what they're saying,' David said. 'That's when someone has told them something which they don't like, and which they probably don't understand.'

Keen to have examined the issue fairly, he explained that a frame of mind in which one dismisses experts is 'not evil necessarily' because 'there's quite a lot I don't understand', but that this reaction is 'a knee-jerk kind of thing' and 'doesn't bear examination for a microsecond'.

★

This was not his only brush with Michael Gove. In 1992, the future Tory politician was one of the presenters of a short-lived TV comedy series called *A Stab in the Dark*, alongside the comedian David Baddiel. In one episode, in the hope of finding evidence that Attenborough was a hypocrite when it came to his stance on the environment, Gove was filmed rifling through Attenborough's dustbins. The most controversial evidence he managed to uncover was that Attenborough had bought some canned wine.

★

Technology has changed the world in so many ways during Attenborough's life, and this includes its influence on the experience of exploration. He takes a nuanced view on this.

'Before mobile phones, if you got into trouble there was only one person who could get you out of it, and that was you,' he said. 'Now if I'm in trouble, I can just phone and ask for someone to come and rescue me.'

For him, this was a mixed bag. He said the era of mobile phones 'makes you take a different attitude, subconsciously changing decisions about where you go and how you behave', making it 'safer' but 'much less liberating'.

He added: 'Until quite recently you were able to get away and leave everything behind, because you didn't have phones. In the rainforest, you were in the same situation as an indigenous hunter.'

But now, 'if you've got a mobile phone you can speak to family and you're probably getting news updates. It changes the way you behave, creating a sense of irresponsibility.'

*

Attenborough has lived in a dramatically changing world. In 2018, he told an interviewer he had become 'aware that there are things you take for granted that your grandchildren don't'.

Asked for an example, he said: 'Privacy, perhaps.'

'I mean social privacy, I don't mean personal privacy. The whole business of communications is now so transformed. What is the social group in which you revolve normally? That is in work or in the family, but it is international for the kids now. For them, it's about self-exposure.'

★

DID YOU KNOW?

Wildlife on One, narrated by Attenborough, was the BBC's flagship natural history programme for nearly 30 years.

Sir David has spoken out on overpopulation – never a topic for the faint-hearted to wade into. 'There are three times as many human beings on this planet than when I first made a television programme,' said Attenborough in 2021.

Showing early signs of the tone of urgency in which he has increasingly spoken, he added: 'This is not something that happened over eons of history. It's right now, and if we don't sort out how we deal with the planet, we're in big trouble.'

*

The end of the world has been depicted so much in movies, television dramas and novels, but Sir David is keen to remind us that the threats to the planet he is concerned about are only too real.

'The planet I saw as a young man has changed beyond recognition,' he said. 'If the Arctic melts, seas will rise and flood cities. This is not H G Wells. It's not science fiction.'

However, he always holds out hope. 'We still have a chance to stop it happening,' he added.

*

The very air we breathe has changed drastically during Attenborough's life. When he was born, in 1926, average

levels of atmospheric carbon dioxide, the greenhouse gas that traps heat and plays an integral part in the greenhouse effect, were roughly 306 parts per million (ppm). By 2022, they had shot up to 417ppm, said researchers from the University of East Anglia.

Attitudes to the environment have also changed radically during Attenborough's life, and he is quick to admit that he has not always been as aware of mankind's effect on nature as he is now.

'As a young man, I felt I was out there in the wild, experiencing the untouched natural world, but it was an illusion,' he said.

'The tragedy of our time has been happening all around us, barely noticeable from day to day – the loss of our planet's wild places, its biodiversity.'

★

He has wondered aloud whether governments have the correct priorities. 'The nature of human beings is that they'd far rather face the disaster that is happening tonight than the one that is happening tomorrow,' he said in 2015.

'Climate change will affect the whole of humanity, while terrorist attacks will only affect a small section of humanity,' he explained, adding that 'humanity is facing a very big, slow, long, drawn-out threat, and that is to do with the way the weather is changing and the size of the population.'

★

Attenborough's remarks on climate have become steadily more urgent as the years have passed. 'The truth is: the natural world is changing,' he said. 'And we are totally dependent on that world. It provides our food, water and air. It is the most precious thing we have and we need to defend it.'

He has said his diet has become increasingly meat-free as he has become aware of the effect that animal agriculture has on the environment.

'I have certainly changed my diet,' he said in 2020. 'Not in a great sort of dramatic way. But I don't think I've eaten red meat for months.'

'I do eat cheese, I have to say, and I eat fish,' he added, 'but by and large I've become much more vegetarian over the past few years than I thought I would ever be.'

'We must change our diet,' he said in his 2020 feature film *A Life on Our Planet*. 'Half of fertile land on Earth is now farmland, 70 percent of birds are domestic, majority chickens. There's little left for the world. We have completely destroyed it.'

In an interview with *Radio Times*, he said: 'The planet can't support billions of meat-eaters. If we all ate only plants, we'd need only half the land we use at the moment.'

Little wonder, then, that he has said: 'I no longer have the same appetite for meat' and 'subconsciously maybe it's because of the state of the planet'.

The world's champion

In 2018, Sir David addressed a UN climate change summit in Poland. His message was clear and stark:

'Right now we are facing a manmade disaster of global scale, our greatest threat in thousands of years: climate change,' he said. 'If we don't take action, the collapse of our civilizations and the extinction of much of the natural world is on the horizon.'

He said: 'The world's people have spoken. Time is running out', and he added: 'Leaders of the world, you must lead. The continuation of civilizations and the natural world upon which we depend is in your hands.'

*

In recent years Attenborough has often been invited to speak at important gatherings, as he became the go-to man for the big occasion.

On World Oceans Day 2017, he delivered a message to 90 heads of state at the opening of the United Nations Ocean Conference. In a grave warning, he told the delegates that the public has taken the ocean for granted, leading to a horrendous reality.

'Now we are facing the consequences: the seas are warming, rising, and becoming more acidic. It's a sobering thought, that coral reefs may be lost within the next century,' he said.

However, true to his approach to environmental advocacy, he assured them that 'the ocean's power

of regeneration is remarkable – if we just offer it the chance'. He added that 'the choice lies with us'.

★

In 2019, he told the World Economic Forum in Davos, Switzerland, that human activity had taken the world into a new era, which could undermine civilization.

'I am quite literally from another age,' he told the prestigious audience. 'I was born during the Holocene – the 12,000 [year] period of climatic stability that allowed humans to settle, farm and create civilizations.'

'In the space of my lifetime, all that has changed,' he continued. 'The Holocene has ended. The Garden of

Eden is no more. We have changed the world so much that scientists say we are in a new geological age: the Anthropocene, the age of humans.'

What would be the best way to address the problems ahead? He had a simple principle for that: 'We need to move beyond guilt or blame, and get on with the practical tasks at hand.'

He left his audience in no doubt as to what was at stake. 'What we do now, and in the next few years, will profoundly affect the next few thousand years,' he said.

★

Attenborough told world leaders at the COP26 climate summit in Glasgow in 2021 that 'young people can give us the impetus we need to rewrite our story' and he warned the assembled leaders that future generations would judge them for their success or failure.

In front of an audience of delegates that included US President Joe Biden, Canadian Prime Minister Justin Trudeau and German Chancellor Angela Merkel, he said the climate emergency 'comes down to a single number: the concentration of carbon in our atmosphere'.

After ten thousand years of stability, conditions were becoming more dangerous and volatile due to human activity, he explained.

'Our burning of fossil fuels, our destruction of nature, our approach to industry, construction and learning are releasing carbon into the atmosphere at an unprecedented pace and scale,' he said. 'We are already in trouble. The stability we all depend on is breaking.'

★

Attenborough has always been at pains to make sure that his message on climate is not delivered in a human-centric tone. Instead, he lays out the harsh realities for all life on Earth. However, in doing so, he underlines the responsibility that humans have for those they share the planet with.

In *Life on Earth*, he says: 'The fact is that no species has ever had such wholesale control over everything on Earth, living or dead, as we now have.'

He continues: 'That lays upon us, whether we like it or not, an awesome responsibility. In our hands now lies not only our own future, but that of all other living creatures with whom we share the earth.'

★

Sir David's voice is certainly one that carries. The producer of *Prehistoric Planet*, Jon Favreau, spoke of the 'magical moments' when the star recorded his narration for the show.

Praising Sir David for nailing the narration in one take, he said: 'It's like having the world's best storyteller reading you a bedtime story of the images that you've spent years creating. It's just absolutely magical.'

*

Attenborough's 2016 series *Planet Earth II* drew to a close with a stirring plea for us to make our planet a welcoming, inhabitable place for all creatures. He spoke about humanity's responsibility while reflecting on the increased urbanity of modern life. The man who spent much of his childhood roaming around the English countryside, and a lot of his adulthood exploring forests and other natural terrains, can see the positives and negatives of city life.

'Now, over half of us live in an urban environment,' he said. 'My home, too, is here in the city of London. Looking down on this great metropolis, the ingenuity with which we continue to reshape the surface of our planet is very striking.'

He continued: 'But it's also sobering. It reminds me of just how easy it is for us to lose our connection with the natural world. Yet it's on this connection that the future of both humanity and the natural world will depend.'

Sir David concluded: 'Surely, it is our responsibility to do everything within our power to create a planet that provides a home not just for us, but for all life on Earth.'

★

Praising Sir David, the *New York Times* said he had transformed 'from a talking and writing crocodile hunter to the greatest living advocate of the global ecosystem'.

★

The effect on viewers was significant, as many people admitted on Twitter. 'Not gonna lie David Attenborough's speech just moved me to tears,' wrote one. 'Shivers, tingles, tears,' tweeted another.

Broadcaster Fearne Cotton tweeted that it was 'the most poignant bit of TV I've seen in a long while', adding that it 'made me weep'. The sports broadcaster and former footballer Gary Lineker said: 'Got to love David Attenborough. Quite possibly the greatest broadcaster of our time.'

*

Attenborough remains committed to the mission of empowering people with knowledge about climate change. At the COP26 UN climate conference in 2021, he touched on the crucial need for greater collective climate action, by laying down the gauntlet for younger generations: 'If working apart we are a force powerful enough to destabilize our planet, surely working together we are powerful enough to save it.'

Sir David continued: 'In my lifetime I've witnessed a terrible decline,' he said. 'In yours, you could and should witness a wonderful recovery.'

*

At a first screening of the 2019 nature series *Seven Worlds, One Planet*, Attenborough offered his advice to a five-year-old in the audience. The boy was too nervous to ask his question when he was handed the microphone, so his father asked on his behalf: 'What can he do to save the planet?'

'You can do more and more and more the longer you live, but the best motto to think about is not waste things,' Attenborough said. 'Don't waste electricity, don't waste paper, don't waste food. Live the way you want to live but just don't waste. Look after the natural world, and the animals in it, and the plants in it too. This is their planet as well as ours. Don't waste them.'

5

The Legacy

National Treasure

Alastair Fothergill has produced several of Attenborough's works, including the series *The Blue Planet* and the film *Deep Blue*. He believes his famous colleague is truly unique. 'What makes him special, apart from all his personal qualities, is the timing of his life' because he has seen so much change in the natural world over the course of that long life.

★

Although he is widely regarded as a national treasure, Attenborough has often shrugged off this status. When asked what being labelled a national treasure means to

him, he said: 'Nothing, except that people are favourably disposed toward you.'

He added: 'You're not being elected, you haven't got the power to become prime minister. The problem is that you are credited with more wisdom and apprehension than is the case – which is quite easy actually. People think you know everything, but of course you don't!'

★

The Australian filmmaker Dr Chadden Hunter worked with Attenborough in shows such as *Planet Earth II* and *Frozen Planet*. He loved how Attenborough had retained his boyish enthusiasm, despite decades in the field.

'Here's a guy who's been working in wildlife filmmaking for over 60 years so would be forgiven for acting like he'd seen it all,' he said. 'And yet when we bring him a new story about some weird parental behaviour in a rarely seen poison dart frog his eyes light up like a toddler at the zoo.'

*

Hunter also shot *Attenborough's Wonder of Eggs,* in the BBC's *Natural World* series, at Imperial College London. Thomas Angus, the college's photographer and image manager, remembered the experience well – and how it exceeded his expectations.

'It's very tempting to gush about how being in the room with David doing his thing would be everything you might imagine,' he said. 'But no, it's so much more, and he was absolutely on point nailing every take first go.'

*

After he made the 2018 show *Dynasties* for the BBC, Attenborough noted that ethologists choose names for animals that 'have no similarity to the names we use for our children and friends' to avoid 'being accused of one of the cardinal sins of ethology – anthropomorphism, that is to say, attributing human characteristics and emotions to an animal without adequate justification'.

However, he added: 'Some degree of anthropomorphism, of course, is justifiable and inevitable. If an elephant, on seeing you, lifts its trunk, flaps its ears and then charges, you are justified, at the very least, in saying that it is angry.'

*

DID YOU KNOW?

Sir David Attenborough is the only person ever to win BAFTAs in black and white, colour and 3D TV.

Sir David was voted Britain's favourite television presenter of all time in 2023, when he won 28 per cent of the vote in the Perspectus Global poll.

The top five were:
1. Sir David Attenborough
2. Sir Terry Wogan
3. Sir Bruce Forsyth

4. Graham Norton

5. Jon Snow

★

Nick Gates, a producer on *Wild Isles*, noted that 'some of the most powerful natural history content has got his name on it' and 'there's something very special about having David Attenborough present a series about the wildlife of Britain and Ireland' because 'it is personal'.

'It has to be personal,' added Gates. 'It's his home. It's our home. If David Attenborough tells us to protect it, it's very powerful.'

★

In a BBC documentary in 2023, Attenborough revealed the discovery of a fossilized pliosaur with a skull the size of a single bed, and teeth like daggers.

This meant, noted *The Times*, that 'perhaps the friendliest face in broadcasting' would 'meet one of prehistory's scariest monsters'.

Asked what the most exotic thing he'd ever eaten was, Attenborough replied: 'Caterpillars, perhaps.'

Fleshing out the point, he said they were 'big moth caterpillars in New Guinea that you put on a fire to burn off the hairs'. He added: 'They come out like Twiglets.'

Although the pace of scientific discovery continues to accelerate, Attenborough said that this does not have a major impact on his work.

'The fact is that the level of scientific insight in these programmes is pitched at sixth-form [16–19-year-olds],' he said. 'It's not as if it's cutting-edge stuff. It's more like here's a duck-billed platypus and it has warm blood and lays eggs. And that doesn't change a lot.'

*

The question of how to replace Attenborough continues to bewilder the world, as Jean-Baptiste Gouyon, associate professor in Science Communication at University College London, observed in 2021.

'Just like a new queen bee has to leave the hive and establish its own colony, for another personality to rise and become as central to wildlife television as David Attenborough is today, wildlife television will have to be reinvented, and different ways of showing nature on TV will have to be found,' he wrote.

*

Interviewers frequently describe him as a passionate and humble man, with a fine line in self-deprecation.

'He is the man you imagine,' wrote science journalist Ed Yong in 2016 in a 'love letter' to Attenborough, published by *The Atlantic*: 'a peerless raconteur, thoughtful and twinkly when talking about wildlife, cantankerous when asked about his own status.'

*

Yong had previously interviewed Attenborough in his living quarters. 'His house was beautiful, furnished by the expected paintings of wildlife and tribal artifacts, a collection of beautiful fossils on a shelf behind his sofa, and more incongruously, an absolutely massive plasma-screen telly,' he wrote.

*

Sir David was once asked what television he likes watching. He said he enjoyed the British versions of *The Office* and *People Like Us* and 'anything that makes me laugh. And I watch natural history programmes – partly because I like 'em. But also to see what people have done. And also because I might be working with the cameraman at some stage, and it's nice to be able to say: "I thought that thing you did with grizzly bears was fantastic."'

However, he added: 'It will be no surprise to you, though, or anybody else, that a lot of contemporary television I don't think well of.'

★

In a *Radio Times* interview to mark his 96th birthday in 2022, Attenborough named his four favourite documentaries he had made:

The Lost Gods of Easter Island (2000)

A Blank on the Map (1971)

Charles Darwin and the Tree of Life (2009)

Lost Worlds, Vanished Lives (1989)

★

Although he has had to have a great deal of patience to get some of the shots needed for a show, Attenborough says that scientists have it much harder because they need to do the same process over and over.

'I remember a very bright guy in Panama who would get up every morning, trek through the forest, find an orchid and sit by it all day to count how many bees visited it,' he said. 'He'd been doing it for months and I think there's a bit of *rite du passage* in it. The senior scientists say: "Well I bloody suffered, so you're going to suffer too."'

★

Attenborough was asked for his favourite place on the planet. He named Far North Queensland in Australia, where he filmed the 2021 TV mini-series *Life in Colour*. He and his team filmed in a variety of locations there, including Lizard Island, Heron Island, North Stradbroke Island, Kuranda, Cairns, Port Douglas, Crater Lakes and Atherton Tableland.

'It has, for a naturalist, everything,' he enthused. 'It has an amazing rainforest, which is quite unlike any other rainforest in the world. Down on the coast it has the Great Barrier Reef. On top of that there's terrific wine and food, so that's the place for me.'

★

When he made a documentary with the Queen in 2018, the two national treasures strolled around the lush gardens of Buckingham Palace. During their walk, he pointed out the impracticality of a sundial's position in the gardens.

'A sundial, neatly planted in the shade,' he said, pointing at it. Amused by the irony of it, the Queen replied: 'Isn't it good, yes?'

The pair, both 91 years of age at the time of the conversation, also looked far into the future when

Attenborough predicted that 'there will be all kinds of different trees growing here in a hundred years, maybe'.

'Might easily be, yes,' the Queen acknowledged, before adding with a smile, 'I won't be here though.'

It was confirmed later that the sundial had been moved out into the sunlight.

★

After the Queen died in 2022, Attenborough said her laughter was her 'most precious' quality.

Although the late monarch sometimes had to laugh politely, 'if there was something funny she laughed in a genuine way', he remembered.

And when the Queen truly laughed, 'she wasn't putting it on and that made it very easy', he added.

★

Following Her Majesty's death, he also remembered what it was like when he worked with her on a documentary entitled *The Queen's Green Planet* in 2018.

During the documentary, the pair strolled around the royal estates and spoke of the challenges of climate change.

'If there was a technical hitch, she wanted to know what it was, and if it had a funny side, she was quick to see the joke,' he said.

'Yet not for one second could you forget that you were in the presence of someone who had willingly accepted enormous responsibility and dedicated her life to serving the nation – that you were, in short, in the presence of royalty.'

★

Sir David attracted a flood of praise on Twitter when *Frozen Planet II* was broadcast just days after the death of Queen Elizabeth II. The programme saw him explore

Antarctica, and feature emperor penguin chicks trying to survive the harsh sea ice.

For many viewers, 60 minutes of content from this wholesome, oddly reassuring man were just the tonic they needed as the nation mourned.

One viewer wrote on Twitter: 'The Queen has died and there's nothing more comforting than watching a David Attenborough documentary.'

Another wrote that 'Sir David Attenborough is just what the nation needs now', adding: 'BBC, you are irreplaceable. I have a feeling Her Majesty would also approve.'

'Watching Sir David Attenborough' is 'the perfect medicine' at such a time, said another, warning that 'the world will never be ready for his passing'.

*

Attenborough has also spoken warmly of the Queen's successor, King Charles III, praising him for being 'at the forefront' of concern about the planet.

'He took quite extreme lines when they were not as popular or as widespread as they are now,' he said of the new monarch.

Charles has sometimes attracted mockery for his habit of talking to houseplants, but for Sir David this is a beautiful practice.

'The question of talking to the plants at the time was joked about but actually now you realize that

that came from his heart – he really meant it – and it couldn't be more important now than it's ever been.'

*

Attenborough has spoken out in support of women's causes but he has declined to declare himself a feminist.

'You'll discover in countries where women have control over their own bodies, where they have education, where they have birth control, where they have facilities and where they are literate, when those things happen, the birth rate falls,' he said. 'Always. Always.'

However, asked if this meant he was a feminist, he said: 'I'm not a feminist. I'm a humanist. I'm neither one side nor the other. It's about the human being. And wanting human beings to be better off so they don't view children as an insurance for the future.'

Inspiring the next generation

In an era when so many people want to become famous and the centre of attention, Attenborough, one of the best-known British people, believes that he should be as little noticed as possible.

'The best thing I can do is to keep out of the way,' he said of his approach to wildlife broadcasting. 'The best thing I can do is keep quiet. People think that the credit in some way belongs to me. It doesn't. It belongs to the natural world, the wonder, and to the connection which comes from the cameramen. That's why the programmes are worth watching. Because the natural world is just full of spectacle and wonder.'

★

Attenborough was named 'the great-grandfather of nature broadcasting' by *The Independent*.

Springwatch presenter Michaela Strachan went one step further, saying he was the 'god of wildlife programmes and presenters'.

Her co-host, Chris Packham, said: 'He told us stories, that's the great thing.'

★

Attenborough remarked to *Time* magazine, at the age of 92: 'I'm very surprised I'm still employed. But I'm just very grateful I am.'

A decade prior to that, he had told *Discover* magazine that there were 'lots' of younger versions of him that he admired and he wondered whether they wanted him out of the way: 'There's no shortage of good people doing what I do and I imagine that there must be queues of them going, "For God's sake, he's been there for fifty years. Why doesn't he put his feet up and give other blokes a chance?"'

He continued: 'All one asks is that they treat the animals with respect and if they treat them with knowledge and admiration then that's a bonus.'

★

The actress Indira Varma was once asked who she had wanted to be when she was a child. 'Growing up,

I wanted to be a clown,' said the *Game of Thrones* star. 'Or a mime artist. Or David Attenborough.'

*

The composer Hans Zimmer is also a fan of Attenborough. The Oscar-winner, who has worked alongside Sir David on a number of projects including *Frozen Planet II*, *Planet Earth II* and *Seven Worlds, One Planet*, said: 'He's not cajoling, he's not crusading, he's just showing you.'

Heaping praise on his collaborator's style, he added: 'He makes you fall in love and like all good love stories, all good love affairs, to treat them mindfully with a little respect.'

*

Sometimes, the kids know best. It took a letter from a young fan to make Attenborough realize what it is that he loves about the animal kingdom.

'I had a sweet letter from a girl who said she liked the programme,' he said. 'She ended the letter by saying

"I like animals because they are very different" and I thought, yeah, she's hit it on the head. That's exactly why I like animals, because they are different.'

★

Sir David made the day of another child when he replied to the boy's letter about dinosaurs. In 2022, six-year-old Theodore Bland, from Yorkshire, wrote to Attenborough using a a dinosaur-printed writing set he had won as a prize at school.

In his letter, he asked Sir David: 'How many T-Rex bones have explorers found?' In a handwritten reply, Sir David told him that he wasn't sure of the exact amount, but it was 'certainly over 100'.

Theo's mother, Katie Bland, said the reply 'really made Theo's day'. She added that her young son 'reminds me daily that he doesn't want to be David Attenborough, he wants to be himself but with the same jobs'.

★

On another occasion in the same year, a four-year-old girl named her new pet, a stick insect, Sir David Stickenborough, and wrote a letter to its famous namesake to tell him.

In his reply, he said: 'Thank you for your letter. I am so glad you are interested in stick insects. I am too and, when I was your age, I also kept some. They are indeed fascinating. There are at least two thousand five hundred different species world-wide. Most come from the tropics and only a few species ever reach this country.'

*

Another heart-warming correspondence came when a four-year-old boy called Otis Allen wrote to ask whether humans would one day be extinct as dinosaurs once were. 'The answer is that we need not do so as long as we look after our planet properly,' Sir David replied, offering hope.

Children from Swanmore Church of England Primary School were delighted when Attenborough replied to their letter, in which they had asked which his favourite nocturnal animal was.

'Dear Children of Year One,' his handwritten reply began. 'Thank you for your letter. My favourite nocturnal animal is a bat. Best wishes, David Attenborough.'

*

When a seven-year-old boy from London called Leo Sordello-Savale watched Sir David's programmes during lockdown, he was inspired to start his own channel on YouTube, which he called 'Leo's Animal Planet'.

One day, he wrote to Attenborough to thank him for his shows and to mention the YouTube channel they had inspired. His mother remembered: 'He sent Leo a letter back thanking him, and saying he had seen this YouTube Channel and to "keep up the good work".'

*

However, it's not just youngsters who are excited when they receive replies from the great man. In 2020, an

81-year-old called Adrian Cutler wrote a poem about global warming and sent it to Attenborough.

He was blown away when he got a handwritten reply. 'Thank you for letting me see your poem,' wrote Attenborough. 'I hope you manage to get it published.'

★

Having spoken about many different topics with confidence and insight, there is one question that continues to bamboozle Sir David. An interviewer for *The Independent* discovered this first-hand when she asked him: what is happiness and how does one achieve it?

'Well I suppose happiness is something one enjoys, but that's . . . Not what you mean . . .' he said. 'The process of getting better,' he continued, 'happiness is very difficult to . . .'

After a pause, he said: 'I suspect that happiness is not a state but rather a transition . . .' Continuing to struggle for a reply, he said: 'You get that bubbling happiness

when you achieve things . . . Self improvement, yes.
No . . . Many things.'

Clearly that's one topic that he's still in the process of
wrapping his head around!

*

When he joined Instagram in 2020, Sir David broke
Friends actress Jennifer Aniston's record for the fastest
time taken to reach a million followers on the picture-
sharing app.

According to Guinness World Records, his follower
count raced to seven figures in just four hours and
44 minutes. The previous year, Aniston had reached the
milestone in five hours and 16 minutes.

In his first Instagram post, he wrote: 'Saving our planet
is now a communications challenge.'

Commenting later on how many followers he had on
Instagram, he said: 'I feel privileged that they should
listen to what an old bloke like me is talking about.'

★

In 2021, Attenborough met members of the royal family at Kensington Palace. Prince Louis, then aged three, asked the broadcaster to name his favourite animal.

'I think I like monkeys best, because they're such fun,' he said. 'They can jump all over the place, and they don't bite, at least . . . some do, but if you're a bit careful they don't bite. And they're so funny, and I like them a lot. Mind you, you can't have monkeys sitting around the home because that's not where they live, they live out in the forest.'

Advanced years

As he reaches ever more advanced years, Attenborough feels torn over his stature, as he explained during an interview with the BBC in 2019.

'It's very odd but the fact remains I've been at it 60 years,' he said. Reflecting upon the scale of his influence on British viewers, he continued: 'You can say nobody under the age of 75 can have been without my voice coming from the corner of the room at various times and that must have an effect.'

He added: 'It's a huge advantage for me because you go there with some sort of reputation and people are aware of you, and in a sense you've been part of the family for quite a long time, which is an extraordinary obligation really and a privilege.'

*

His producer, Alastair Fothergill, said that he had noticed the effect that Attenborough had on the public, saying: 'He's got the celebrity of a Beckham.'

He remembered being there when Attenborough appeared on stage in front of ten thousand people in Regent's Park, London, in 2001, introducing a BBC Prom concert of music from *The Blue Planet*.

'When David went on there was this extraordinary cheer – pop star adulation. It seemed to set him back a bit,' said Fothergill. 'He said, "Hello, I'm David

Attenborough." And there was a noise from the audience, as if to say, "Yeah, like we didn't know." '

*

In 2016 and 2018, Sir David came top in British surveys of the dream dinner-party guest, and in 2017 he was named in a Scottish survey as being the Scots' ultimate dinner-party guest. In 2021, Attenborough, Her Majesty the Queen and Jeremy Clarkson were named as the three top dream dinner-party guests. These were among countless opinion polls from which Sir David has emerged heroically.

Here are some other studies that have picked him out for praise:

In 2006: He was voted the nation's most important cultural icon, just ahead of the singer Morrissey.

In 2011: He was voted Britain's greatest living national treasure.

In 2012: He was the top choice for the British people's 'dream boss'.

In 2014: He was named the UK's most trustworthy figure.

In 2016: He was named as one of the most passionate people in Britain.

In 2017: A survey named him as the famous person they'd most like to share a road trip with.

In 2018: He was the UK's top choice to be on the next £20 note and also voted as the nation's favourite voice, as well as the most admired person in the UK.

In 2019: He was named the most trusted celebrity to recommend a used car and the top choice as subject of a movie biopic.

In 2020: He was voted the owner of Britain's Best Voice, ahead of Joanna Lumley and Stephen Fry, and named as the celebrity most British people wanted as prime minister.

In 2021: Along with Prince William, he was the most popular choice for head of state were the monarchy to be abolished.

In 2023: He was chosen as Britain's favourite TV presenter of all time.

*

In 2013, at the age of 87, he had a pacemaker fitted to regulate his heart. However, this did nothing to regulate his approach to life because, he said, 'retirement would be so boring'.

'If I was earning my money by hewing coal I would be very glad indeed to stop,' he explained. 'But I'm not. I'm swanning round the world looking at the most fabulously interesting things. Such good fortune.'

★

In 2019, as he approached yet another birthday, Attenborough brought a lump to many people's throats when he spoke about the future, saying he couldn't 'bear' to think about it.

'I'm just coming up to 93, and so I don't have many more years around here,' he said. 'I find it difficult to think beyond that because the signs aren't good.'

★

Speaking about death, Attenborough was asked by *Radio Times* whether he believed in an afterlife, or whether he expected to see 'pearly gates'. He replied 'no' to each question.

Asked whether he expected to see a 'kindly old man with a beard', he chuckled and said: 'I should be so lucky. No. Nothing like that.'

*

Someone once asked whether he had to carefully tailor his image, to avoid controversy. He said: 'Well, I think we all wish to be well thought of.' Is there anyone in the public eye better thought of than Sir David?

*

As he advanced in years, Attenborough increasingly came to terms with the fact that his end was coming. His attitude to his mortality was less emotional and more scientific and analytical.

'I think about my own mortality every day,' he told an interviewer. 'And not in a morbid kind of way, but I suppose in an observational kind of way.'

He continued: 'You suddenly realize you aren't remembering proper names any more and whereas three years ago you could tread water in the conversation long enough for the name to come up and move on, you now know there is no point.'

However, he noted that 'dear friends' and 'relatives' were unable to remember anything or 'even walk, poor people'. He said: 'I can't believe I'm as lucky as I am.'

★

Launched in 1923, *Radio Times* has been the nation's key television bible throughout Attenborough's career. In 2023, ahead of his *Wild Isles* documentary, it paid tribute to him, saying: 'No man has opened our eyes to more wonders of the natural world than Sir David Attenborough.'

References

Introduction

p. 2, 'a species that is increasingly . . .': https://www.radiotimes.com/documentaries/louis-theroux-meets-david-attenborough-to-talk-global-warming-animal-kinship-and-mortality/

p. 3, 'I can't believe I've been . . .': https:// www.mirror.co.uk/tv/tv-news/sir-david-attenborough-ill-keep-6721477

p. 3, 'I just point at things': https://www.theatlantic.com/science/archive/2016/05/every-episode-of-david-attenboroughs-life-series-ranked/480678/

p. 4, 'There will never be another . . .': https://www.theguardian.com/tv-and-radio/2019/oct/22/david-attenborough-climate-change-bbc

1. The Making of David Attenborough

p. 13, 'like the Queen, he has . . .': https://www.theguardian.com/tv-and-radio/2019/oct/22/david-attenborough-climate-change-bbc

p. 13, 'An awful lot of people . . .': https://www.thetimes.co.uk/article/the-magazine-interview-sir-david-attenborough-92-on-getting-new-knees-the-queen-and-why-todays-children-need-to-reconnect-with-nature-tbj7xg5gb

p. 15, Clegg had education in her: https://www.pressreader.com/uk/the-daily-telegraph-saturday/20050924/282918085848057

p. 15, 'a staircase': https://www.theguardian.com/lifeandstyle/2011/may/14/david-attenborough-interview#:~:text=Tell%20us%20a%20secret.,as%20well%20as%20ice%2Dcream.

p. 15, 'He got fed up with . . .': https://historyproject.org.uk/sites/default/files/HP0190%20David%20Attenborough%20-%20Transcript.pdf

p. 16, 'I think that every child' . . . *'What were those funny things? . . .'*: http://edition.cnn.com/TRANSCRIPTS/1609/02/ampr.01.html

p. 17, 'keeping tanks of tropical fish' . . . *'venturing across northern England on . . .'*: https://www.theguardian.com/tv-and-radio/2019/oct/22/david-attenborough-climate-change-bbc

p. 17, 'Fossils have fascinated me for' . . . *'collecting the ammonites that are'* . . . *'The excitement of hitting a . . .'*: https://www.tes.com/magazine/archive/mr-lacey-sir-david-attenborough

p. 18, 'As a child I was' . . . *'All kids have that potential . . .'*: *New Life Stories* by David Attenborough (London: HarperCollins, 2011), or David Attenborough's Life Stories, https://www.bbc.co.uk/sounds/play/b00n5w39

p. 19, 'For as long as I' . . . *'the quiet, studious one . . .'*: https://www.theguardian.com/film/2000/oct/27/culture.features1

p. 20, 'I remember my time as . . .': https://www.scouts.org.uk/about-us/our-people/scout-alumni/

p. 21, He suggested to his father: https://web.archive.org/web/20140222033240/http://www.leicestermercury.co.uk/Picture-day-12-Leicester-celebs-famous/story-20596134-detail/story.html

p. 21, 'You could walk up and . . .': https://www.shropshirestar.com/news/uk-news/2020/01/10/sir-david-attenborough-highlights-rare-specimen-closer-to-home/

p. 22, In 2023, an interview with: https://www.bbc.co.uk/news/uk-england-leicestershire-65469567

p. 22, David's younger brother, John, was: https://www.bfi.org.uk/features/remembering-richard-attenborough

p. 24, The architect who designed Haydon: https://www.idealhome.co.uk/news/david-attenboroughs-childhood-home-sale-178720

pp. 24-25, 'as a hero' . . . *'For God's sake look after'* . . . *'People always talked about the* . . .': https://www.thetimes.co.uk/article/sir-david-attenborough-heads-north-to-fulfil-a-childhood-dream-ddzkjnlhvqh

p. 25, 'gurgling brook and the kingfisher' . . . *'That's the landscape I grew* . . .': https://studsterkel.wfmt.com/programs/interview-david-attenborough?t=2833.22%2C2855.9990000000003&a=ISeeThat%2CWateIsSwee

p. 26, 'For me, there is no . . .': https://www.bbc.co.uk/news/science-environment-24839299

p. 26, 'When I was a boy' . . . *'I was away for three* . . .': https://www.dailymail.co.uk/femail/article-2569361/Sir-David-Attenboroughs-childhood-memories.html

p. 27, 'I was climbing the cliff' . . . *'It was when I was* . . .': https://www.theguardian.com/lifeandstyle/2011/may/14/david-attenborough-interview#:~:text=Tell%20us%20a%20secret.,as%20well%20as%20ice%2Dcream.

p. 28, 'Getting lost': https://www.timeout.com/london/the-big-interview-sir-david-attenborough

p. 28, 'When she showed interest in' . . . *'In those days you only* . . .': https://www.dailymail.co.uk/femail/article-2569361/Sir-David-Attenboroughs-childhood-memories.html *pp. 29–30, 'bowled over by the man's'* . . . *'the idea that mankind was . . .'*: https://www.bfi.org.uk/features/remembering-richard-attenborough

p. 30, 'I wish the world was . . .': https://www.bbc.co.uk/newsround/51131823

p. 31, 'My parents were great supporters . . .': https://www.independent.co.uk/news/people/profiles/education-passed-failed-david-attenborough-1161070.html

p. 32, 'everyone of military age was' . . . *'I was astonished even then . . .'*: https://www.tes.com/magazine/archive/mr-lacey-sir-david-attenborough

p. 32, 'Primary school teachers have got . . .': https://www.thetimes.co.uk/article/david-attenborough-interview-on-chatham-house-prize-climate-change-greta-thunberg-and-becoming-a-fishetarian-ztgmdfz73

p. 33, 'Young people – they care': https://insidetime.org/barack-obama-meets-david-attenborough/

pp. 33–35, 'Good work, spoilt by silly' . . . *'There was so much rote'* . . . *'with gusto'* . . . *'not in the least interested'* . . . *'sheer infectious enthusiasm made me'* . . . *'It was my first opportunity . . .'*: https://www.tes.com/magazine/archive/mr-lacey-sir-david-attenborough

p. 35, 'If you were extremely bright . . .': https://www.independent.co.uk/news/people/profiles/education-passed-failed-david-attenborough-1161070.html

p. 36, 'His name was J R Cottrill' . . . *'a good amateur dramatic society . . .'*: https://www.tes.com/magazine/archive/mr-lacey-sir-david-attenborough

p. 37, As the brothers grew up: interview with Michael Attenborough CBE, recorded for University of Leicester: https://www.leicestermercury.co.uk/news/leicester-news/michael-attenborough-reveals-exclusive-insight-5665300

p. 37, 'It's great that the series . . .': https://www.theguardian.com/tv-and-radio/2023/apr/02/tourists-arrive-skomer-attenborough-wild-isles-wales

p. 38, 'I cannot tell you just . . .': https://staffblogs.le.ac.uk/specialcollections/2016/05/09/glimpses-of-the-young-david-attenborough-in-the-university-archives/

p. 38, 'I am personally interested because . . .': https://staffblogs.le.ac.uk/specialcollections/2016/05/09/glimpses-of-the-young-david-attenborough-in-the-university-archives/

pp. 39–40, 'I picked it up and' . . . 'You are the most brilliant . . .': speech given at Bradgate Park, Leicester, to launch an appeal by the local Rotary Club: https://www.independent.co.uk/news/people/sir-david-attenborough-confesses-i-cheated-on-my-biology-exam-a486501.html

p. 40, 'I regret that I must . . .': https://www.bbc.co.uk/news/uk-england-leicestershire-36258694

p. 41, RRS Sir David Attenborough: https://www.bas.ac.uk/polar-operations/sites-and-facilities/facility/rrs-sir-david-attenborough/

p. 42, 'My stock-in-trade is . . .': https://www.radiotimes.com/tv/documentaries/louis-theroux-meets-david-attenborough-to-talk-global-warming-animal-kinship-and-mortality/

p. 42, Frederick and Mary organized committees: https://www.bfi.org.uk/features/remembering-richard-attenborough

p. 42, 'It is just an indication . . .': https://
www.telegraph.co.uk/tv/2023/03/10/
sir-david-attenborough-last-great-adventure-bbc-wild-isles/

p. 43, 'It felt surprisingly warm and' . . . 'hard to imagine a more . . .':
https://www.pbs.org/wgbh/nova/transcripts/3305_jewel.html

*p. 44, 'If it's not health and' . . . 'the interaction between humans
and . . .'*: https://www.dailymail.co.uk/news/article-5980345/
Sir-David-Attenborough-says-health-safety-gone-mad-
stopping-UK-children-enjoy-nature-outdoors.html

2. Hitting the Small Screen

p. 46, The Friends of Richmond Park: https://www.frp.org.uk/
our-achievements/

p. 46, In 2023, he planted an: https://www.royalparks.org.uk/
media-centre/press-releases/sir-david-attenborough-plants-a-
tree-for-a-new-woodland-in-richmond-park-to-honour-the-
late-queen-elizabeth-ii

*pp. 46–47, 'At the end of World' . . . 'dutifully got a scholarship' . . .
'as it were eavesdropping . . .'*: https://historyproject.org.uk/sites/
default/files/HP0190%20David%20Attenborough%20-%20
Transcript.pdf

p. 47, The trait David most dislikes: https://www.theguardian.
com/lifeandstyle/2011/may/14/david-attenborough-
interview#:~:text=Tell%20us%20a%20secret.,as%20well%20
as%20ice%2Dcream

*pp. 47–48, 'didn't cut too many corners' . . . 'If you read science,
you' . . . 'I found the three-dimensional . . .'*: https://www.
independent.co.uk/news/people/profiles/education-passed-
failed-david-attenborough-1161070.html

p. 48, At Cambridge, he came across: https://www.philanthropy.
cam.ac.uk/give-to-cambridge/expeditions-society-cuex

p. 49, 'I thought I cannot go . . .': https://historyproject.org.uk/sites/
default/files/HP0190%20David%20Attenborough%20-%20
Transcript.pdf

p. 49, 'working in a factory during . . .': https://www.theguardian.
com/lifeandstyle/2011/may/14/david-attenborough-
interview#:~:text=Tell%20us%20a%20secret.,as%20well%20
as%20ice%2Dcream.

p. 50, 'My job there was footling . . .': https://historyproject.org.uk/
sites/default/files/HP0190%20David%20Attenborough%20-%20
Transcript.pdf

p. 50, 'dismal' . . . 'depressed' . . . 'And it was then . . .': *Life on Air* by
David Attenborough (London: BBC Books, 2002)

p. 52, 'inexpressibly boring because it took . . .': https://historyproject.
org.uk/sites/default/files/HP0190%20David%20Attenborough%
20-%20Transcript.pdf

p. 52, 'embryonic city gent . . .': *Life on Air* by David Attenborough
(London: BBC Books, 2002)

p. 52, 'It's the same kind of . . .': https://historyproject.org.uk/sites/
default/files/HP0190%20David%20Attenborough%20-%20
Transcript.pdf

*p. 53, 'absolutely horrified' . . . 'crouching underneath the desk,
saying' . . . 'I thought it was absolutely' . . . 'I'm a married man, I . . .'*:
https://historyproject.org.uk/sites/default/files/HP0190%20
David%20Attenborough%20-%20Transcript.pdf

p. 54, 'finally abandoned': *Life on Air* by David Attenborough
(London: BBC Books, 2002)

pp. 54–55, 'no surprise' . . . 'the author of an authoritative' . . . 'no identifiable qualifications for their . . .': Life on Air by David Attenborough (London: BBC Books, 2002)

p. 55, He estimates his pay for: https://historyproject.org.uk/sites/default/files/HP0190%20David%20Attenborough%20-%20Transcript.pdf

p. 58, Other animal output came courtesy: *Adventures of a Young Naturalist* by David Attenborough (London: Two Roads, 2017) (originally published as *The Zoo Quest Expeditions: Travels in Guyana, Indonesia and Paraguay* [Lutterworth Press, 1980])

p. 59, 'jobbing producer' . . . 'music recitals, archaeological quizzes, political . . .': Adventures of a Young Naturalist by David Attenborough (London: Two Roads, 2017) (originally published as *The Zoo Quest Expeditions: Travels in Guyana, Indonesia and Paraguay* [Lutterworth Press, 1980])

p. 60, 'extraordinary studios, which looked to . . .': https://historyproject.org.uk/sites/default/files/HP0190%20David%20Attenborough%20-%20Transcript.pdf

p. 60, 'emotionally [w]rung out. It was' . . . 'Paul went back to his . . .': https://historyproject.org.uk/sites/default/files/HP0190%20David%20Attenborough%20-%20Transcript.pdf

p. 61, 'internal BBC politics': https://www.independent.co.uk/news/uk/david-attenborough-chris-packham-british-africa-british-isles-b2269393.html

p.61, 'There was a chap trying' . . . 'Eventually we had a meeting . . .': https://www.telegraph.co.uk/tv/2023/03/10/sir-david-attenborough-last-great-adventure-bbc-wild-isles/

p. 62, 'I loathe getting on an airplane' . . . *'I always think when I . . .'*: *New Life Stories* by David Attenborough (London: HarperCollins, 2011)

pp. 63–64, 'exciting scientific discovery' . . . *'relief'*: https://www. google.co.uk/books/edition/Life_on_Air/po4Es1kztr8C?hl=en& gbpv=1&dq=david+attenborough+life+on+air+read+online&pr intsec=frontcover

p. 65, 'The days of the finger-snapping . . .': *Life on Air* by David Attenborough (London: BBC Books, 2002)

pp. 65–66, 'wide smile' . . . *'Texan drawl'* . . . *'I had become interested in'* . . . *'When I heard them, I'* . . . *'Alan was very enthusiastic and'* . . . *'She left her banjo under . . .'*: Interview with BBC producer Julian May in *Songlines Magazine*, edition #125: https://www.songlines.co.uk/ features/sir-david-attenborough-reveals-his-musical-inspirations

p. 68, 'Cos when I take 'em' . . . *'Attenborough is an intelligent young . . .'*: https://www.telegraph.co.uk/culture/ tvandradio/12115518/Sir-David-Attenborough-I-was-kept-off-TV-because-my-teeth-were-too-big.html

p. 69, 'If Auntie did exist, she . . .': *Life on Air* by David Attenborough (London: BBC Books, 2002)

p. 69, 'very good hostess' . . . *'a pair of old slacks'*: *Life on Air* by David Attenborough (London: BBC Books, 2002)

p. 70, One of Attenborough's early shows . . .: https://genome.ch.bbc. co.uk/dfa73ee03e0c4207942f0e98f39d9e24

p. 70, While filming Animal Patterns *in*: *Life on Air* by David Attenborough (London: BBC Books, 2002)

p. 72, 'incredulous delight': *Adventures of a Young Naturalist*
by David Attenborough (London: Two Roads, 2017)
(originally published as *The Zoo Quest Expeditions:
Travels in Guyana, Indonesia and Paraguay* [Lutterworth
Press, 1980])

p. 72, Zoo Quest *debuted on*: https://www.bbc.com/
historyofthebbc/anniversaries/december/zoo-quest/

p. 73, Attenborough enjoyed his trip to: Interview with
BBC producer Julian May in *Songlines Magazine*,
edition #125: https://www.songlines.co.uk/features/
sir-david-attenborough-reveals-his-musical-inspirations

p. 74, After its debut in 1954: *Life on Air* by David Attenborough
(London: BBC Books, 2002)

p. 75, 'You wouldn't see the damn' . . . *''Ello Dave, are
we or . . .'*: Interview with Sandi Toksvig, for BAFTA,
2018: https://www.bafta.org/media-centre/transcripts/
natural-history-with-sir-david-attenborough

p. 76, 'I felt history throbbing around' . . . *'"Shall I address the
people'* . . . *'Eventually I think I said . . .'*: https://historyproject.
org.uk/sites/default/files/HP0190%20David%20Attenborough%
20-%20Transcript.pdf

p. 77, 'consisted of an expert from' . . . *'He talked about them
while . . .'*: https://www.bbc.co.uk/blogs/tv/2012/11/david-
attenborough-collection.shtml

pp. 77–78, 'They are deliberately programmes where' . . . *'There's a
place for all . . .'*: *New Life Stories* by David Attenborough (London:
HarperCollins, 2011)

p. 79, 'We drank a little beer' . . . *'wily and sagacious'*: https://bscine.
com/bsc-members/?id=156

p. 80, There was a stand-off: *Life on Air* by David Attenborough (London: BBC Books, 2002)

pp. 80–81, 'astonished' . . . *'It's impossible, we shot in'* . . . *'At its best it's as . . .'*: https://www.bbc.co.uk/news/entertainment-arts-36091147

pp. 81–82, 'I really, really hate rats' . . . *'I've handled deadly spiders, snakes . . .'*: *David Attenborough's Life Stories*, BBC Radio 4 (April 2011): https://www.bbc.co.uk/sounds/play/b010fd8x

pp. 82–83, 'I was out there filming' . . . *'out in the bush, animals'* . . . *'irrational horror of them . . .'*: https://www.walesonline.co.uk/lifestyle/david-attenborough-im-petrified-rats-1820290#

pp. 83–85, 'Music takes me back to' . . . *'In the day we filmed'* . . . *'These tracks remind me of'* . . . *'Bali then was almost unaffected'* . . . *'I recorded a group with'* . . . *'We used some of it . . .'*: Interview with BBC producer Julian May in *Songlines Magazine*, edition #125: https://www.songlines.co.uk/features/sir-david-attenborough-reveals-his-musical-inspirations

p. 87, When he appeared on the: https://www.bbc.co.uk/programmes/b01b8yy0

p. 88, In 1957, his luxury was: https://www.bbc.co.uk/programmes/p009y8xh

p. 88, In 1979, his favourite piece: https://www.bbc.co.uk/programmes/p009mxny

p. 89, He must have made quite: https://www.independent.ie/style/celebrity/celebrity-news/kirsty-young-sir-david-attenborough-is-my-favourite-desert-island-discs-guest-35392828.html

p. 89, 'I see film of myself . . .': Interview with BBC producer Julian May in *Songlines Magazine*, edition #125: https://www.songlines.co.uk/features/ sir-david-attenborough-reveals-his-musical-inspirations

pp. 89–90, 'I went to his shelter' . . . 'This marked their coming into . . .': Interview with BBC producer Julian May in *Songlines Magazine*, edition #125: https://www.songlines.co.uk/features/ sir-david-attenborough-reveals-his-musical-inspirations

p. 90: 'the wonderful David Attenborough': https://www.nme.com/ news/music/brian-may-8-1253915

p. 91, 'The thing about a bushbaby . . .': https://metro.co.uk/2013/01/29/ david-attenborough-im-not-an-animal-lover-3370670/

p. 91, 'You could just turn up . . .': https://www.telegraph.co.uk/ news/earth/earthnews/9771535/Attenborough-to-wage-war-on- annoying-camera-tricks.html

p. 92, In 1958, he first met: https://www.rct.uk/collection/2014266/ royal-children-at-t-v-studios

p. 93, However, the tables were turned: http://www.ukgameshows. com/ukgs/Animal,_Vegetable,_Mineral

p. 93, 'undoubtedly' . . . 'He played outrageously to the . . .': https://the-past.com/feature/david-attenborough-what-in-the- world-and-mortimer-wheeler/

p. 95, 'I didn't think they were . . .': *Life on Air* by David Attenborough (London: BBC Books, 2002)

p. 97, 'the bugger will bite me': https://www.scotsman.com/ arts-and-culture/books/book-review-life-on-air-by-david- attenborough-2461445 *p. 97, 'cold welcome'* . . . *'professors and fossils seemed an* . . .': https://unesdoc.unesco.org/ark:/48223/pf0000068909

p. 97, 'a sound, full-bodied, vintage . . .': C A Lejeune, *The Observer* (18 January 1953), quoted on Wikipedia

p. 98, 'Mr David Attenborough, aged 38' . . . *'Mr Attenborough, brother of Richard'* . . . *'rather dimly'* . . . *'not privy'* . . . *'on the friendliest terms'*: https://www.thetimes.co.uk/tto/archive/article/1965-03-05/6/1.html

p. 99, Prior to landing the gig: https://www.theguardian.com/culture/2009/sep/26/david-attenborough-interview

p. 99, 'Are you a broadcaster or' . . . *'there was no point in* . . .': https://historyproject.org.uk/sites/default/files/HP0190%20David%20Attenborough%20-%20Transcript.pdf

pp. 99–100, 'greeted with scepticism' . . . *'he was considered lightweight, a'* . . . *'Everybody forgot I wasn't just* . . .': https://www.theguardian.com/tv-and-radio/2019/oct/22/david-attenborough-climate-change-bbc

p. 100, 'absolutely at rock bottom and . . .': https://historyproject.org.uk/sites/default/files/HP0190%20David%20Attenborough%20-%20Transcript.pdf

p. 100, 'art and architecture, literature and . . .': https://www.theguardian.com/artanddesign/2016/may/19/kenneth-clark-civilisation-bbc-review

pp. 101–02, 'should like to extend the' . . . *'the success which I have'* . . . *'I am afraid that, at'* . . . *'We would feel, other things* . . .': https://www.radiotimes.com/tv/entertainment/terry-wogans-unseen-1965-rejection-letter-from-david-attenborough-and-sir-davids-reaction-50-years-on/

p. 103, 'one of the greatest and . . .': https://www.radiorewind.co.uk/radio1/terry_wogan_page.htm

p. 103, 'Good Lord! He wrote asking . . .': https://www.radiotimes.com/tv/entertainment/terry-wogans-unseen-1965-rejection-letter-from-david-attenborough-and-sir-davids-reaction-50-years-on/

p. 103, He added that, even though: https://www.bbc.co.uk/news/entertainment-arts-35530842

p. 104, 'One of the scars on' . . . 'Look, we have to build' . . . 'So can't you please find' . . . 'That doesn't mean to say . . .': https://www.telegraph.co.uk/culture/tvandradio/10784285/David-Attenborough-my-regrets-over-wiping-Alan-Bennett-dross.html

p. 105, In 1960, Attenborough produced and: https://www.bbc.co.uk/iplayer/episodes/p00xjs70/the-people-of-paradise

pp. 106–07, 'voices, attitudes and opinions that' . . . 'Your own say . . . in your' . . . 'presented by a group of' . . . 'Reality is a substitute for . . .': https://www.telegraph.co.uk/tv/0/open-door-when-psychics-racists-anarchists-dressed-gorilla-suits/

p. 107, 'What is striking now is . . .': https://www.theguardian.com/media/2023/jan/24/black-teachers-trans-women-cleaners-cons-the-bbcs-open-door

p. 108, 'We need to think about' . . . 'We still haven't got an . . .': https://www.theguardian.com/tv-and-radio/2019/oct/22/david-attenborough-climate-change-bbc

pp. 109–10, 'I had one of the' . . . 'Look, I don't want you' . . . 'was quite right, of course' . . . 'He and I, only, in . . .': https://www.wimbledon.com/en_GB/news/articles/2017-07-01/qa_sir_david_attenborough.html

p. 110, 'Anybody who invested in a . . .': https://www.wimbledon.com/en_GB/news/articles/2017-07-01/qa_sir_david_attenborough.html

p. 111, Snooker did not take off: *Deep Pockets: Snooker and the Meaning of Life* by Brendan Cooper (London: Constable, 2023)

p. 111, The idea was streamlined by: https://www.bbc.co.uk/blogs/genome/entries/c6d9695f-f7f8-4faa-ab1c-0b1a1c4818fd

pp. 112–13, 'Nobody else had got colour' . . . 'there was a great hoo-hah' . . . 'paying people to go and . . .': https://www.wimbledon.com/en_GB/news/articles/2017-07-01/qa_sir_david_attenborough.html

p. 113, In the 1967 Wimbledon Men's: https://www.wimbledon.com/en_GB/news/articles/2017-07-01/attenborough_force_behind_colour_revolution.html

p. 113, 'I heard the West Germans' . . . 'I was as proud as . . .': https://www.radiotimes.com/tv/sport/tennis/david-attenborough-reveals-how-wimbledon-helped-britain-beat-the-germans-to-colour-tv/

p. 114, 'But now I just write . . .': https://www.theguardian.com/tv-and-radio/2019/oct/22/david-attenborough-climate-change-bbc

3. The Broadcasting Titan

pp. 115–16, 'it's difficult to believe it' . . . 'Television has told the world . . .': https://www.bucksfreepress.co.uk/bestofbucks/national/18932641.sir-david-attenborough-praises-power-television-rose-dor-awards/

p. 117, 'realized that, though you can' . . . 'It occurred to me that . . .': https://www.nytimes.com/1975/11/24/archives/producer-of-tribal-eye-unmasks-society-through-art-and-artifacts.html *p. 118, 'Pythonesque, illuminated manuscript title sequence . . .':* https://web.archive.org/web/20090827065546/http://www.forteantimes.com/features/articles/101/attenboroughs_fabulous_animals.html

p. 118, The first series of Planet: https://www.nme.com/news/david-attenborough-planet-earth-3-100-1913325

p. 119, 'There are some four million . . .': http://www.infocobuild.com/books-and-films/nature/life-earth/episode-13.html

p. 119, 'I think it added to . . .': https://www.theguardian.com/environment/2009/nov/02/david-attenborough-life-on-earth-soundtrack

p. 120, The Life on Earth *book':* https://www.theguardian.com/books/2018/oct/12/life-on-earth-david-attenborough-review

p. 120, 'Why should there be such . . .': https://eden.uktv.co.uk/eden-heroes/sir-david-attenborough/article/more-sir-david-attenborough-quotes/#:~:text=200%20years%20ago%2C%20a%20man,His%20name%20was%20Charles%20Darwin.

p. 121, Attenborough, who has covered the: https://butterfly-conservation.org/about-us/our-president-sir-david-attenborough

p. 121, During the filming of an: https://www.theguardian.com/tv-and-radio/shortcuts/2016/may/04/attenborough-90-wildlife-legend-top-10-tv-moments

p. 121, 'Our planet, the Earth, is . . .': The Living Planet documentary series (BBC, 1984)

p. 122, 'The difficulties are not actually . . .': The Making of The Living Planet documentary film (BBC, 1984)

pp. 123–24, 'One thing that distinguishes men' . . . 'Somewhat shy and not always' . . . 'He enjoys this rather strange . . .': The Making of The Living Planet documentary film (BBC, 1984)

p. 124, David Attenborough is thought to: https://www.shortlist. com/news/david-attenborough-facts

p. 125, 'She did, and gave my' . . . 'The focus of my life,' . . . 'You accommodate things . . .you deal . . .': Life on Air by David Attenborough (London: BBC Books, 2002)

p. 126, 'I coped by working': Life on Air by David Attenborough (London: BBC Books, 2002)

p. 126, 'I would rather have people . . .': https://www.bbc.co.uk/ programmes/b00pdjmk

p. 127, 'In moments of great grief . . .': https://www.stylist.co.uk/ entertainment/celebrity/best-david-attenborough-quotes/33686

p. 127, 'It seems to me that . . .': 'How Many People Can Live on Planet Earth?', *Horizon* (BBC2, 2009)

p. 128, 'I don't think an understanding . . .': https:// www.theguardian.com/tv-and-radio/2012/jan/29/ david-attenborough-desert-island-discs

p. 128, 'Dick was a marvellous comic' . . . 'You know, we just sat . . .': https://www.mirror.co.uk/tv/tv-news/ david-attenborough-brother-richard-hilarious-4432413

p. 128, 'The arts are not a . . .': https://www.dailymail.co.uk/news/ article-2998741/Stars-pack-Westminster-Abbey-Richard-Attenborough-memorial-including-brother-David-Sir-Michael-Caine-Dame-Judi-Dench.html

p. 129, 'I couldn't bear to watch . . .': https://www.mirror.co.uk/tv/ tv-news/david-attenborough-brother-richard-hilarious-4432413

pp. 129–30, 'to ingratiate themselves to the . . .'That wouldn't impress me at' . . . 'It would. I can show . . .': https://www.telegraph.co.uk/women/life/sir-david-attenboroughs-10-best-quotes-about-women/

p. 131, 'Throw a boot at it!' . . . 'Even if he stung you' . . . 'Well, you can if you . . .': Interview on *The Jonathan Ross Show* (2013; ITV1): https://www.express.co.uk/celebrity-news/450515/Sir-David-Attenborough-reveals-he-s-had-a-pacemaker-fitted

p. 132, 'Aneeshwar, I would like you . . .': https://www.mirror.co.uk/tv/tv-news/simon-cowell-surprises-bgt-viewers-27143669

p. 132, Just months later, the BBC's: https://www.birminghammail.co.uk/news/showbiz-tv/bbc-strictly-come-dancing-fans-25336397

p. 132, 'The voice is like a . . .': https://www.telegraph.co.uk/culture/4729076/What-comes-naturally.html

p. 132, The producers of his television: https://www.theguardian.com/tv-and-radio/2023/mar/04/new-david-attenborough-series-about-uk-likely-to-be-his-last-on-location

p. 133, 'We wrote him a letter . . .': https://bravewords.com/news/nightwish-were-turned-down-by-conservationist-david-attenborough-it-was-very-impressive-that-a-man-of-his-stature-would-write-to-us-and-explain-that-he-just-didnt-have-the-time-says-floor-jansen

pp. 133–34, 'Really? Will Adele be cross' . . . 'I think Adele would probably' . . . 'The year is 2015. The' . . . 'delicate and finely tuned animal' . . . 'The weather is poor and . . .': https://www.standard.co.uk/showbiz/celebrity-news/

sir-david-attenborough-provides-the-perfect-narration-to-adele-s-music-video-for-hello-a3105486.html

p. 135, 'Watch as the alpha female' . . . *'The alpha female's job is . . .'*: Radio 1 interview with Greg James, 2014: https://www.theguardian.com/media/2014/feb/19/sochi-2014-bbc-david-attenborough-curling

p. 135, A rave in Birmingham: https://www.birminghammail.co.uk/whats-on/music-nightlife-news/david-attenborough-themed-rave-might-23694736

pp. 136–37, 'It's jolly nice someone of' . . . *'We had no idea what'* . . . *'You're in absolute comfort, you're'* . . . *'we've got cameras pointing from . . .'*: https://www.theguardian.com/media/mediamonkeyblog/2015/nov/25/david-attenborough-dive-bbc-great-barrier-reef#:~:text=Sir%20David%20Attenborough%20was%20as,%E2%80%9Csitting%20in%20an%20armchair%E2%80%9D.

pp. 137–38, 'People say to me, "What' . . . *'whopping great book'* . . . *'there's a chance here, boy'* . . . *'My impression of course is . . .'*: https://www.radiotimes.com/travel/david-attenborough-revisits-the-great-barrier-reef-and-does-a-record-breaking-submarine-dive/

p. 138, 'I think the most alarming . . .': https://www.independent.co.uk/news/people/profiles/sir-david-attenborough-interview-the-one-question-about-life-that-still-baffles-him-10007797.html

p. 139, 'I nominate going to look . . .': https://www.theguardian.com/tv-and-radio/2019/oct/19/just-dont-waste-david-attenborough-advice-bbc-seven-worlds-one-planet#:~:text=%E2%80%9CYou%20can%20do%20more%20and,but%20just%20don't%20waste.

p. 140, 'You can't talk about the . . .': https://www.telegraph.co.uk/tv/2016/11/06/david-attenborough-his-five-funniest-moments/

p. 141, 'You can say to Martyn . . .': https://www.telegraph.co.uk/culture/4729076/What-comes-naturally.html

p. 141, 'fly under my own volition': https://www.theguardian.com/lifeandstyle/2011/may/14/david-attenborough-interview#:~:text=Tell%20us%20a%20secret.,as%20well%20as%20ice%2Dcream.

p. 143, 'absurd creature': https://www.wired.com/2013/11/absurd-creature-of-the-week-quetz/

p. 143, 'wonderful, flying monsters': https://www.theguardian.com/lifeandstyle/2011/may/14/david-attenborough-interview#:~:text=Tell%20us%20a%20secret.,as%20well%20as%20ice%2Dcream

p. 143, 'There are some circumstances where . . .': https://www.telegraph.co.uk/culture/4729076/What-comes-naturally.html

p. 143, There have been no end: https://www.theguardian.com/tv-and-radio/shortcuts/2016/may/04/attenborough-90-wildlife-legend-top-10-tv-moments

p. 145, 'being the breeding season . . .': https://www.standard.co.uk/showbiz/celebrity-news/david-attenborough-at-90-five-funniest-moments-from-unimpressed-sloths-to-amorous-birds-and-adele-a3242331.html

p. 145, 'A man, who is drunk . . .': https://www.digitalspy.com/tv/a514433/sir-david-attenborough-reveals-his-scariest-animal/

p. 146, 'rude to count': https://www.bbc.co.uk/newsround/23144921

p. 146, 'honorary degrees are just about' . . . 'That's something that's out of . . .': https://www.thetimes.co.uk/article/

the-magazine-interview-sir-david-attenborough-92-on-getting-new-knees-the-queen-and-why-todays-children-need-to-reconnect-with-nature-tbj7xg5gb

p. 147, 'We were in Borneo' . . . 'One said, "I want to . . ."': https://www.mirror.co.uk/tv/tv-news/david-attenborough-lost-words-face-25446268

p. 148, 'He was, as one would' . . . 'I came away feeling I'd' . . . 'If I do have regrets . . .': https://www.radiotimes.com/tv/documentaries/louis-theroux-meets-david-attenborough-to-talk-global-warming-animal-kinship-and-mortality/

p. 149, 'Give him a glass of' . . . 'Actually, I've given up chocolate' . . . 'eating too much of it': https://www.radiotimes.com/tv/documentaries/louis-theroux-meets-david-attenborough-to-talk-global-warming-animal-kinship-and-mortality/

p. 149, 'Take it! Just do it': https://www.radiotimes.com/tv/documentaries/louis-theroux-meets-david-attenborough-to-talk-global-warming-animal-kinship-and-mortality/

p. 149, 'chastised' . . . 'private vote': https://www.thetimes.co.uk/article/david-attenborough-interview-on-chatham-house-prize-climate-change-greta-thunberg-and-becoming-a-fishetarian-ztgmdfz73

p. 150, 'A look is enough. Like . . .': https://www.telegraph.co.uk/tv/2023/03/10/sir-david-attenborough-last-great-adventure-bbc-wild-isles/

p. 150, In 2019, a YouGov poll: https://yougov.co.uk/topics/entertainment/articles-reports/2018/11/07/david-attenborough-most-popular-person-britain

pp. 150, 152, 'slug porn' . . . 'features extra lashings of sex' . . . 'magical pendulum of love' . . . 'We put a lot of . . .': https://

inews.co.uk/news/wild-isles-producers-animal-sex-david-attenborough-bbc-slug-2228063

p. 151, he'd be a sloth: https://www.huffingtonpost.co.uk/david-attenborough-reddit-ama_n_568d5e36e4b0a2b6fb6e4ab0

p. 151, 'I don't feel it with . . .': https://www.radiotimes.com/tv/documentaries/louis-theroux-meets-david-attenborough-to-talk-global-warming-animal-kinship-and-mortality/

p. 152, So many Chinese viewers downloaded: https://www.theguardian.com/tv-and-radio/2019/oct/22/david-attenborough-climate-change-bbc

p. 153, 'Children now don't write to . . .': https://www.telegraph.co.uk/tv/2023/03/10/sir-david-attenborough-last-great-adventure-bbc-wild-isles/

pp. 153–54, 'substantial effect' . . . 'I think that increasing public . . .': https://www.telegraph.co.uk/news/2023/02/15/david-attenborough-has-made-people-interested-plants-study-finds/

p. 154, 'led the world on an' . . . 'He taught the world to . . .': https://www.theguardian.com/commentisfree/2010/nov/05/david-attenborough-first-life-television

p. 155, 'A lot of my friends . . .': https://www.thetimes.co.uk/article/i-preferred-my-early-work-recalls-david-attenborough-9s9j96n99

p. 155, 'I would be perfectly happy . . .': https://www.thetimes.co.uk/article/sir-david-attenborough-on-blue-planet-ii-making-enemies-and-why-he-has-no-plans-to-quit-9t6796gzf

p. 156, 'Good, workable knees': https://www.theguardian.com/lifeandstyle/2011/may/14/david-attenborough-interview

p. 156, 'I'm fantastically lucky. I can . . .':
https://www.telegraph.co.uk/tv/2023/03/10/
sir-david-attenborough-last-great-adventure-bbc-wild-isles/

*pp. 156–57, 'His hair has been whipped' . . . 'When he notices a
KitKat . . .':* https://www.telegraph.co.uk/men/thinking-man/
david-attenborough-at-90-i-think-about-my-mortality-every-
day/?WT.mc_id=tmgoff_psc_ppc_performancemax_dyn
amiclandingpages&gclid=EAIaIQobChMIyZ2uo8vx_
QIVZWHmCh2kJQS2EAMYASAAEgJMhvD_BwE

p. 158, 'There are around 67 steep . . .': https://www.theguardian.
com/tv-and-radio/2023/mar/04/new-david-attenborough-series-
about-uk-likely-to-be-his-last-on-location

*pp. 159–60, 'If you sit David close' . . . 'We thought, "Wow
that could' . . . 'If David gets it he' . . . 'although everyone
was happy':* https://www.liverpoolecho.co.uk/news/tv/
sir-david-attenborough-could-died-26406597

*p. 160, 'We're doing a film in' . . . 'the insurance people
wouldn't do . . .':* https://www.mirror.co.uk/tv/tv-news/
david-attenborough-hang-glider-wildlife-2962716

*pp. 160–61, 'phenomenal barometer of change' . . . 'If you look at
the . . .':* https://www.theguardian.com/tv-and-radio/2023/
mar/04/new-david-attenborough-series-about-uk-likely-to-be-
his-last-on-location

*p. 161, 'ultimate goal' . . . 'veritable dream come true' . . . 'lying in
a damp field . . .':* https://www.terramater.at/news/behind-the-
scenes-illuminating-work-with-sir-david-attenborough/

p. 162, 'I have had the fortune . . .': https://eden.uktv.co.uk/
eden-heroes/sir-david-attenborough/article/more-sir-
david-attenborough-quotes/#:~:text=200%20years%20

ago%2C%20a%20man,His%20name%20was%20Charles%20 Darwin.

p. 163, 'the longest career as a . . .': https://www. guinnessworldrecords.com/world-records/longest-career-as- a-television-naturalist#:~:text=The%20longest%20career%20 as%20a,Television%20on%202%20September%201953.

4. Protector of the Planet

pp. 165–66, 'Chimpanzees can show great kindness' . . . 'We are the most inventive . . .': https://eden.uktv.co.uk/eden-heroes/ sir-david-attenborough/article/more-sir-david-attenborough- quotes/#:~:text=200%20years%20ago%2C%20a%20 man,His%20name%20was%20Charles%20Darwin.

p. 166, 'striking' . . . 'how similar they are to . . .': https://www. youtube.com/watch?v=IFACrIx5SZ0

pp. 167–68, 'achieved things that many of' . . . 'I think everyone is grateful . . .': https://www.insider.com/greta-thunberg-david- attenborough-interview-skype-call-2019-12

p. 169, 'visionary environmentalist': https://www.thenationalnews. com/world/uk-news/2022/06/08/sir-david-attenborough- awarded-prestigious-second-knighthood/

p. 169, 'efforts to inform about, and . . .': https://news.sky.com/ story/sir-david-attenborough-nominated-for-nobel-peace-prize- along-with-pope-francis-the-who-and-alexei-navalny-12530137

p. 170, As the Norwegian nominators have: https://www.bbc.co.uk/ news/av/world-63170356

p. 170, 'biggest of compliments that you . . .': https://www.atlasobscura.com/articles/

heres-every-living-or-extinct-creature-named-after-david-attenborough

p. 170, At the last count, more: https://en.wikipedia.org/wiki/List_of_things_named_after_David_Attenborough_and_his_works

p. 170, 'There is something very calming . . .': https://www.mirror.co.uk/tv/tv-news/attenborough-90-celebrates-amazing-life-7914719

p. 171, 'I can't actually remember taking . . .': https://www.telegraph.co.uk/travel/safaris-and-wildlife/perfect-planet-behind-scenes-david-attenboroughs-breathtaking/?WT.mc_id=tmgoff_psc_ppc_generic_articles_travel&gclid=EAIaIQobChMIkeXCpPqm_gIVwevtCh1tdABjEAMYASAAEgLDOvD_BwE

p. 172, 'a cloying, anthropomorphizing sentiment': https://www.theguardian.com/media/2006/nov/04/broadcasting.weekendmagazine

pp. 172–73, 'delighted' . . . 'Having visited several times, I' . . . 'Long-term studies like this . . .': https://www.jackfm.co.uk/hits/news/oxfordshire-news/sir-david-attenborough-praises-oxfords-great-tit-count-at-wytham-woods/

p. 173, 'many people are having a' . . . 'I am lucky. I have . . .': https://www.bbc.co.uk/news/entertainment-arts-54317603

p. 174, 'Nature once determined how we . . .': https://speakola.com/ideas/david-attenborough-launch-hbo-our-planet-2019

pp. 174–75, 'a few short years' . . . 'In this film, we'll meet' . . . 'just enough remains of the . . .': https://www.aol.co.uk/entertainment/sir-david-attenborough-warns-few-230100056.html?guccounter=1&guce_referrer=aHR0cHM6Ly93d3cuZ29vZ2xlLmNvbS88&guce_referrer_sig=AQAAANCWGn_SboYBw_

MuOEeln_oS0QHzBksravTD62JeJppYo8ODPuhRGT-
LB9P5f9INEHThjx3_
piSjSUPmYqqw1kBD0YQO4NWjSxytCob6a0vnQD_
tYvHokPJx8Cfl4xydtcdXcd1TbRI20CFcbN-
ZIwsjdJJ3qAXdgBcMe2ciebjR

pp. 175–76, 'be curbed' . . . *'We are going to have'* . . . *'We've
had time to sit . . .'*: https://www.bbc.co.uk/news/
science-environment-54268038

p. 176, 'cheering all by myself' . . . *'I filmed a year
or . . .'*: https://www.thesun.co.uk/news/13521078/
there-are-3-times-as-many-humans-on-the-planet-than-when-
i-started-tv-we-have-a-problem-says-sir-david-attenborough/

p. 177, 'had enough of experts' . . . *'That's a cry from somebody'* . . . *'not
evil necessarily'*: https://www.independent.co.uk/climate-change/
news/david-attenborough-brexiteers-spit-europeans-eu-leave-
uk-bbc-michael-gove-experts-a7967591.html

p. 178, This was not his only: https://www.theneweuropean.co.uk/
brexit-news-a-stab-in-the-dark-when-michael-gove-rifled-
through-34064/

pp. 178–79, 'Before mobile phones, if you' . . . *'makes you take a
different'* . . . *'Until quite recently you were'* . . . *'if you've got a
mobile . . .'*: https://www.dailymail.co.uk/news/article-8111239/
Sir-David-Attenborough-issues-stark-warning-societys-
dependence-mobiles.html

pp. 179–80, 'aware that there are things' . . . *'Privacy, perhaps'* . . .
'I mean social privacy, I': https://www.thetimes.co.uk/article/
the-magazine-interview-sir-david-attenborough-92-on-getting-
new-knees-the-queen-and-why-todays-children-need-to-
reconnect-with-nature-tbj7xg5gb

p. 180, 'There are three times as . . .': https://www.telegraph.co.uk/travel/safaris-and-wildlife/perfect-planet-behind-scenes-david-attenboroughs-breathtaking/?WT.mc_id=tmgoff_psc_ppc_generic_articles_travel&gclid=EAIaIQobChMIkeXCpPqm_gIVwevtCh1tdABjEAMYASAAEgLDOvD_BwE

p. 181, 'This is not something that . . .': https://www.thesun.co.uk/news/13521078/there-are-3-times-as-many-humans-on-the-planet-than-when-i-started-tv-we-have-a-problem-says-sir-david-attenborough/

p. 181, 'The planet I saw as' . . . 'We still have a chance . . .': https://www.telegraph.co.uk/travel/safaris-and-wildlife/perfect-planet-behind-scenes-david-attenboroughs-breathtaking/

p. 181, The very air we breathe: https://www.discoverwildlife.com/people/david-attenborough-climate-change/

p. 183, 'As a young man, I' . . . 'The tragedy of our time . . .': https://www.discoverwildlife.com/people/david-attenborough-climate-change/

p. 183, 'The nature of human beings' . . . 'Climate change will affect the . . .': https://www.independent.co.uk/news/people/profiles/sir-david-attenborough-interview-the-one-question-about-life-that-still-baffles-him-10007797.html

p. 184, 'The truth is: the natural . . .': https://wwf.org.au/blogs/10-best-nature-quotes-from-sir-david-attenborough/?rd=1

pp. 184–85, 'I have certainly changed my' . . . 'I do eat cheese, I' . . . 'We must change our diet' . . . 'The planet can't support billions' . . . 'I no longer have the . . .': https://plantbasednews.org/news/environment/is-david-attenborough-vegan/

pp. 185–86, 'Right now we are facing' . . . *'The world's people have spoken . . .'*: https://www.theguardian.com/environment/2018/dec/03/david-attenborough-collapse-civilisation-on-horizon-un-climate-summit

p. 186, 'Now we are facing the . . .'the ocean's power of regeneration . . .': https://www.bbcearth.com/news/attenboroughs-message-for-world-oceans-day

pp. 187–88, 'I am quite literally from' . . . *'In the space of my'* . . . *'We need to move beyond'* . . . *'What we do now, and . . .'*: https://www.theguardian.com/tv-and-radio/2019/jan/21/david-attenborough-tells-davos-the-garden-of-eden-is-no-more

pp. 188–89, 'young people can give us' . . . *'comes down to a single'* . . . *'Our burning of fossil fuels . . .'*: Speech by Attenborough at COP26 climate conference in Glasgow in 2021: https://www.heraldscotland.com/politics/19686352.humanity-already-trouble-climate-change-warns-sir-david-attenborough/

p. 190, 'The fact is that no' . . . *'That lays upon us, whether . . .'*: *Life on Earth* by David Attenborough (London: William Collins Sons/BBC Books, 1979)

pp. 190–91, 'magical moments' . . . *'It's like having the world's . . .'*: https://www.radiotimes.com/tv/documentaries/prehistoric-planet-producer-magic-david-attenborough-moment-exclusive-newsupdate/

pp. 191–92, 'Now, over half of us' . . . *'But it's also sobering. It'* . . . *'Surely, it is our responsibility . . .'*: https://www.independent.co.uk/arts-entertainment/tv/news/planet-earth-2-finale-final-episode-watch-sir-david-attenborough-a7469371.html

p. 192, 'from a talking and writing . . .': https://www.nytimes.com/2018/05/29/books/review/david-attenborough-adventures-of-a-young-naturalist.html *pp. 192–93, 'Not gonna lie David Attenborough's'* . . . *'Shivers, tingles, tears'* . . . *'the most poignant bit of'* . . . *'Got to love David Attenborough'*: https://www.dailyedge.ie/david-attenborough-planet-earth-2-speech-3133751-Dec2016/

p. 193, 'If working apart we are' . . . *'In my lifetime I've witnessed . . .'*: Speech by Attenborough at COP26 climate conference in Glasgow in 2021: https://www.heraldscotland.com/politics/19686352.humanity-already-trouble-climate-change-warns-sir-david-attenborough/

p. 194, 'What can he do to' . . . *'You can do more and . . .'*: https://www.theguardian.com/tv-and-radio/2019/oct/19/just-dont-waste-david-attenborough-advice-bbc-seven-worlds-one-planet#:~:text=%E2%80%9CYou%20can%20do%20more%20and,but%20just%20don't%20waste.

5. The Legacy

p. 195, 'What makes him special, apart . . .': https://www.theguardian.com/tv-and-radio/2019/oct/22/david-attenborough-climate-change-bbc

p. 196, 'Nothing, except that people are' . . . *'You're not being elected, you . . .'*: https://www.gq-magazine.co.uk/article/david-attenborough-trump

p. 197, 'Here's a guy who's been . . .': https://www.news.com.au/entertainment/tv/behind-the-scenes-of-david-attenboroughs-documentaries/news-story/3645703bd437a413d178d2fad2e42849

p. 198, 'It's very tempting to gush . . .':https://blogs.imperial.ac.uk/photography/2018/03/31/behind-scenes-david-attenborough/

pp. 198–99, 'have no similarity to the' . . . *'Some degree of anthropomorphism . . .'*: Foreword by David Attenborough to *Dynasties: The Rise and Fall of Animal Families* by Stephen Moss (London: BBC Books, 2018), companion book to Attenborough's 2018 BBC series *Dynasties*

p. 199, Sir David was voted Britain's: https://www.dailymail.co.uk/news/article-11837133/David-Attenborough-voted-Britains-favourite-TV-presenter-time.html

p. 200, 'some of the most powerful' . . . *'It has to be personal'*: https://www.theguardian.com/tv-and-radio/2023/mar/04/new-david-attenborough-series-about-uk-likely-to-be-his-last-on-location

p. 200, 'perhaps the friendliest face in . . .': https://www.thetimes.co.uk/article/david-attenborough-to-reveal-sea-predator-with-head-the-size-of-a-bed-pnf0b28m6

p. 201, 'Caterpillars, perhaps' . . . *'big moth caterpillars in New . . .'*: https://www.discovermagazine.com/planet-earth/an-interview-with-david-attenborough

p. 202, 'The fact is that the . . .': https://www.discovermagazine.com/planet-earth/an-interview-with-david-attenborough

p. 202, 'Just like a new queen . . .': https://theconversation.com/why-david-attenborough-cannot-be-replaced-152193

p. 203, 'He is the man you . . .': https://www.theatlantic.com/science/archive/2016/05/every-episode-of-david-attenboroughs-life-series-ranked/480678/

p. 203, 'His house was beautiful, furnished . . .': https://www.discovermagazine.com/planet-earth/an-interview-with-david-attenborough

pp. 203–04, 'anything that makes me laugh' . . . *'It will be no surprise . . .'*: https://www.telegraph.co.uk/culture/4729076/What-comes-naturally.html

p. 204, In a Radio Times *interview*: https://www.radiotimes.com/tv/documentaries/attenborough-at-90-sir-david-attenborough-picks-his-favourite-four-documentaries/

p. 205, 'I remember a very bright . . .': https://www.discovermagazine.com/planet-earth/an-interview-with-david-attenborough

p. 206, 'It has, for a naturalist . . .': David Attenborough Acceptance Speech, 2017 Britain-Australia Society Award at Australia House in London: https://awol.com.au/sir-david-attenborough-favourite-place/59204#:~:text=My%20favourite%20place%20is%20North,Barrier%20Reef%2C%E2%80%9D%20he%20continued.

pp. 207–08, 'A sundial, neatly planted in' . . . *'there will be all kinds'* . . . *'Might easily be, yes'*: https://www.womanandhome.com/life/royal-news/sweet-resurfaced-video-highlights-queens-quick-witted-response-to-david-attenboroughs-joke-about-shaded-sundial-at-buckingham-palace/

p. 208, 'most precious' . . . *'if there was something funny'* . . . *'she wasn't putting it on . . .'*: https://www.itv.com/news/2022-09-09/her-laugh-was-the-most-precious-thing-david-attenborough-mourns-the-queen

p. 209, 'If there was a technical' . . . *'Yet not for one second . . .'*: https://royalcentral.co.uk/uk/a-tribute-to-the-queen-from-her-friend-sir-david-attenborough-180693/

pp. 210–11, 'The Queen has died and' . . . *'Sir David Attenborough is just'* . . . *'Watching Sir David Attenborough . . .'*: https://virginradio.co.uk/tv-film/75028/

sir-david-attenboroughs-frozen-planet-ii-praised-for-bringing-comfort-after-the-queens-death

p. 211, 'at the forefront'... 'He took quite extreme lines'... 'The question of talking to...': https://uk.news.yahoo.com/david-attenborough-says-king-charles-110534064.html

p. 212, 'You'll discover in countries where'... 'I'm not a feminist. I'm...': https://www.independent.co.uk/news/people/profiles/sir-david-attenborough-interview-the-one-question-about-life-that-still-baffles-him-10007797.html

p. 213, 'The best thing I can...': https://www.independent.co.uk/arts-entertainment/tv/news/david-attenborough-95-birthday-funniest-moments-b1843607.html

p. 213, 'the great-grandfather of nature broadcasting': https://www.independent.co.uk/arts-entertainment/tv/news/david-attenborough-95-birthday-funniest-moments-b1843607.html

p. 213, 'god of wildlife programmes and'... 'He told us stories, that's...': https://www.bbc.co.uk/news/entertainment-arts-36242216

p. 214, 'I'm very surprised I'm still...': https://time.com/5560233/david-attenborough-climate-documentary-netflix/

p. 214, 'lots'... 'There's no shortage of good'... 'All one asks is that...': https://www.discovermagazine.com/planet-earth/an-interview-with-david-attenborough

p. 214, 'Growing up, I wanted to...': https://www.theguardian.com/lifeandstyle/2022/jun/04/i-wanted-to-be-a-clown-or-david-attenborough

p. 215, 'He's not cajoling, he's not'... 'He makes you fall in...': https://www.hamhigh.co.uk/things-to-do/national/23066507.hans-zimmer-praises-sir-david-attenborough-makes-fall-love/

p. 215, 'I had a sweet letter . . .': https://www.dailymail.co.uk/news/article-2929240/What-favourite-animal-s-nine-month-old-baby-says-David-Attenborough.html

p. 216, 'How many T-Rex bones have' . . . 'really made Theo's day': https://www.thescarboroughnews.co.uk/news/people/sir-david-attenborough-delights-young-scarborough-dinosaur-enthusiast-with-letter-3927923

p. 217, 'Thank you for your letter': https://scoop.upworthy.com/sir-david-attenborough-sends-a-heartwarming-response-to-a-child-who-named-her-new-pet-after-him

p. 217, 'The answer is that we . . .': https://www.bbc.co.uk/news/uk-wales-56429104

p. 218, 'Dear Children of Year One': https://www.portsmouth.co.uk/education/david-attenborough-surprises-pupils-at-swanmore-primary-school-with-a-hand-written-note-4011008

p. 218, 'He sent Leo a letter . . .': https://www.standard.co.uk/news/london/london-kid-climate-change-david-attenborough-cop26-camberwell-b961524.html

p. 219, 'Thank you for letting me . . .': https://www.portsmouth.co.uk/news/people/gosport-great-grandfather-gets-letter-from-sir-david-attenborough-after-sending-global-warming-poem-2936586

p. 219, 'Well I suppose happiness is' . . . 'I suspect that happiness is . . .': https://www.independent.co.uk/news/people/profiles/sir-david-attenborough-interview-the-one-question-about-life-that-still-baffles-him-10007797.html

p. 220, 'Saving our planet is now' . . . 'I feel privileged that they . . .': https://www.bbc.co.uk/news/entertainment-arts-54292947

p. 221, 'I think I like monkeys . . .': 'Ask David Attenborough',
released by Kensington Palace

*pp. 221–22, 'It's very odd but the' . . . 'It's a huge advantage
for . . .':* https://www.ladbible.com/entertainment/
tv-and-film-david-attenborough-says-young-peoples-obsession-
with-him-is-odd-20191020

p. 222, 'He's got the celebrity of' . . . 'When David went on there . . .':
https://www.telegraph.co.uk/culture/4729076/What-comes-
naturally.html

*pp. 225–26, 'retirement would be so boring' . . . 'If I
was earning my . . .': Radio Times,* quoted on https://
www.theguardian.com/tv-and-radio/2013/sep/10/
david-attenborough-human-evolution-stopped

p. 226, 'bear' . . . 'I'm just coming up to . . .': https://metro.
co.uk/2019/04/27/david-attenborough-admits-doesnt-long-live-
must-protect-costs-9328814/

*pp. 226–27, 'pearly gates' . . . 'kindly old man with a' . . . 'I should
be so lucky':* https://www.radiotimes.com/tv/documentaries/
louis-theroux-meets-david-attenborough-to-talk-global-
warming-animal-kinship-and-mortality/

p. 227, 'Well, I think we all . . .': https://www.radiotimes.com/tv/
documentaries/louis-theroux-meets-david-attenborough-to-
talk-global-warming-animal-kinship-and-mortality/

*pp. 227–28, 'I think about my own' . . . 'You suddenly realize
you aren't' . . . 'dear friends':* https://www.telegraph.
co.uk/men/thinking-man/david-attenborough-at-
90-i-think-about-my-mortality-every-day/?WT.
mc_id=tmgoff_psc_ppc_performancemax_dyna
miclandingpages&gclid=EAIaIQobChMIyZ2uo
8vx_QIVZWHmCh2kJQS2EAMYASAAEgJMhvD_BwE

p. 228, *'No man has opened our . . .'*: https://www.radiotimes.com/tv/documentaries/david-attenborough-radio-times-new-issue-cover/

About the author

Chas Newkey-Burden writes about animal rights, veganism and the environment for the *Guardian, Independent,* the *i, Metro* and the *Daily Telegraph.*

He is the author of dozens of books, including *Running: Cheaper Than Therapy, The Runner's Code, Get Lucky: Rituals, Habits and Superstitions of the Rich and Famous* and *The Reduced History of Dogs.*

Acknowledgements

Thanks to Nicola Crane, for asking me to write this book. Thanks also to Louisa Johnson, Faye Robson and Alison Wormleighton for all your wisdom and support. Thanks to Chris and Harry for bolstering me.